HOW T

PEOPLE

Analyzing The
Narcissistic Mother

Jason Browne

This document is geared towards providing exact and reliable information in regards to the topic and issue covered. The publication is sold with the idea that the publisher is not required to render accounting, officially permitted or otherwise qualified services. If advice is necessary, legal or professional, a practiced individual in the profession should be ordered.

- From a Declaration of Principles which was accepted and approved equally by a Committee of the American Bar Association and a Committee of Publishers and Associations.

The information provided herein is stated to be truthful and consistent, in that any liability, in terms of inattention or otherwise, by any usage or abuse of any policies, processes, or directions contained within is the solitary and utter responsibility of the recipient reader. Under no

CONTENTS

INTRODUCTION

We all express ourselves in unique ways. This uniqueness is our personality and what makes us individuals. In essence, our intellect, emotions, and mannerisms all combine together to form our personality. This manner of expression is our idiosyncrasy. So there's absolutely nothing wrong with having a personality. Actually, it's impossible not to have a personality.

However, personality can go overboard. It can cross the line. When this is the case, we call it a personality disorder. You see, our personality can draw people closer to us or piss the heck out of them and push them away. Personality becomes disorderly when it persistently and rigidly brings discomfort to others—and even to oneself.

Personality disorders are more prevalent in our society today than many realize. Continuous research and common instances of familial abuse, especially maternal, are proof. This is where the title of this book comes in: *The Psychology of a Narcissistic Mother.* Parenting is an interesting and life-shaping experience, which can make this world a better place or a terrible place to be. It's indisputable that parents, especially moms, play a great role in the upbringing of children.

Parents are there to protect and guide their children, and nurture and cherish them. They are there to instill positivity into them. Simply put: parents are there to be there for their children. The moment any of these ideals is missing, there's a very serious issue, which shouldn't be taken with a pinch of salt.

Let's be very clear about this from the outset: no mom in her sane mind would ever harm her child, hate her child, envy her child, or abuse her child in any way. What many don't realize is that behind the wall of every maternal abuse—or, indeed, abuse of any kind—is a personality disorder. And the earlier we all understand this, the better for us all.

I've been privileged to hear firsthand information from those who've suffered horrifying abuse from their moms. And you know what? These people are still toughing out the pain they've gone through. Ninety-eight percent of those who confided in me about their moms' abuse are women—and all of them are married with kids now. Isn't that interesting!

Though they are okay now in other areas, the childhood pain just won't go away. They've undergone various therapies and used different tricks—and they're gradually healing—but they are all still plowing through the rough childhood experiences they had with their moms.

This book is the result of anecdotal evidence and intense personal empirical studies on NPD. Because I know that I can't possibly cover everything about Narcissistic Personality Disorder (NPD) in this book, I've compiled helpful sources at the end of this book in case you want to know more about this personality disorder. You're welcome!

I admit that personality disorders (PDs) are generally still obscure. They're obscure in the sense that several research projects are still ongoing. Besides, scholars disagree on the categories of PDs and the extent of a personality disorder. This obscurity is aided by the fact that PDs are mental conditions that are primarily diagnosed based on observation and questioning.

Nonetheless, PDs are real and can be diagnosed. With the aid of much research and modern examination, PDs have been named and grouped into categories based on their primary characteristics. For instance, NPD is so named because narcissism is the prevalent behavior. So also is Paranoid Personality Disorder, which has paranoia as its prevalent behavior.

Knowledge is power, goes the timeless saying. This book, be assured, will practically guide you on what NPD is, and is not, its causes, management, impact, and, most importantly—how to recognize it in yourself and others. By arming yourself with the knowledge you'll acquire in this book, you'll be a lifesaver to hundreds—perhaps thousands—of people.

You'll be better positioned to help victims of NPD to heal, by giving them advice and tips you'll learn in this book, or by even buying it for them. And never know, you could even end up helping those with NPD! My ultimate aim for this book is to create awareness of narcissism. Kindly note, this book is a guide and should be used as such.

CHAPTER ONE

WHAT IS NARCISSISTIC PERSONALITY DISORDER (NPD)?

The word "Narcissism" you most likely understand, but you probably aren't so sure about Narcissistic Personality Disorder (NPD). I know this term can be intimidating because of its jargon-like tone, but I'll make a very good attempt to explain what it means. In fact, this entire chapter will be devoted to what NPD is and recognizing it primarily in your mom and in other people.

As the name implies, and in the simplest of terms, NPD is a mental health issue that affects the behavioral pattern of those who have it. But that's still not a very helpful definition. So let's break it down some more. We have a very helpful definition from *Wiktionary*, which defines NPD as a personality disorder characterized largely by an overinflated sense of self-importance typically caused by unbalanced parental valuation during childhood.

Yes, that's more like it! We are getting closer to cracking this terminology. You see, NPD isn't all about an overinflated ego or fragile self-worth. *Webster Dictionary* agrees, but adds that people with NPD are persistently in need of admiration, lack empathy for others, have excessive pride in their achievements, and are snobbish, disdainful, or patronizing.

In the true sense of it, these characterizations are all linked together. The person who's full of herself will definitely not accept criticism. She'll lack empathy for others because she's proud and doesn't give a darn about anyone. She'll be condescending because of her larger-than-life ego. She'll be full of herself. She won't care about the feelings of others or what they're going through.

(Please, allow me to use *she* for the sake of consistency and the subject of this book, "mom." Thank you!)

A narcissist (a person with NPD) only understands one person's point of view—hers. Whatever she does is right in her own eyes, and God help the person who tells her she's wrong. I believe you're beginning to get the picture now. You're beginning to see the character traits of a person with NPD. Sometimes, some words are best explained, not defined. Even lexicologists and experts recognize this necessity.

The problem isn't in having a sense of self-importance or inspiring ego, as we all have and should have, but it's in going off the scale. In NPD, the person has an ultra-dose of self-importance. Her logic is subservient to her ego. This is the problem! Character flaws and antisocial tendencies are bound to surface the moment logic is dominated by ego.

Of course, ego has its own big part to play, but it has to work hand-in-hand with reality. This brings us to another aspect of NPD: the world of fantasy. People with NPD live in a fantasy world. In this nonexistent world, they are very powerful, successful, and highly intelligent. This is the reason those with NPD see themselves as superior and unique, and why they expect to be worshiped and adored. When they feel they aren't worshiped or given the attention they need, they can misbehave and cause chaos. This isn't good for anyone.

I know you're eager to jump right to where I address NPD and motherhood, but I'll address it soon. Just a few more words to go, and we'll get there. But it's really important that I lay down the nuances before then. You wouldn't want your hamburger without beef, right? I thought so!

Once you understand the symptoms of NPD, you'll be able to recognize the signs in anyone who has it, including your mom—and even in yourself. One of the big problems, if not the biggest, a person with NPD has is living in real life. She sees herself as the sovereign Queen of a Utopian world, where she's adored and loved and unchallenged. This is her world; one of endless privileges and entitlements.

So, and understandably, she gets irked when she's denied her supposed rights. Her eyes turn angry when she's challenged and questioned. She'll never forgive you for criticizing her. Trust me; she'll surely repay you generously in the offing. Do you know why? Well, because you've stepped on the wrong snake, you've hurt the feelings of the leader of a great nation in a mental world, and her minions will definitely come for your head.

You must have realized by now that a person living with NPD will have problems in many areas of life. She'll struggle with her relationships, career, and finances. She'll struggle to keep her friends, but she'll easily make enemies. She'll struggle to parent her child. In short, she'll have many struggles. You get the point?

Unrealistic expectations from people will frustrate a person with NPD. When she expects her child or partner or friend to do something, and they don't do it, she'll take offense at their supposed inaction, for daring to disobey her. There's a high probability that that person who always expects you to do something, whether it's realistic or not, has NPD.

People with NPD may also be poor in handling finances, and the reason isn't so puzzling. How do you expect a very rich and powerful person in some unknown world to be prudent with money? What do you expect from a person who feels she's immune to our financial laws and principles? People suffering from NPD will find it difficult to be provident with their resources.

People without NPD see the world from a self-to-others perspective, but people with NPD see the world from a self-to-self perspective. Everything revolves around them. Of course, we all see the world through our own eyes. While this is true, people without NPD see the world with their eyes opened to reality. But a person living with NPD sees the world with her eyes closed to reality. This is a fundamental difference.

Healthy living requires healthy relationships with others and personal comfort shouldn't be at the cost of anyone else.

There must be a balance but people with NPD don't see it that way. They see themselves in themselves. There's no selflessness in their world.

This isn't right, and that's why it's called a disorder. It's not a normal state of mental being.

Since it's a disorder, people living with NPD need to seek medical treatment. They need to be saved from harming others and even themselves. Though people with NPD may look bold and intimidating on the outside, they're quite fragile on the inside. As a matter of fact, their mental state is fragile. Everything about them is fragile. They build castles of fragile imaginations and live in them, so they have fragile expectations of others.

Behind the mask of their self-importance and ostentation is delicate self-esteem that fears criticism and ridicule, assumed or real. They will do anything to hide this vulnerability, but it's like a flame that can't be hidden. It will surely show in the way they behave.

Recognizing the Signs and Behaviors

It's about time we dug into the main point of this book. But before we proceed, I strongly feel I have to explain why we are focusing on moms. The title of this book could've prompted you to wonder why it's a mom we're considering and not a dad. The reason for this isn't to slight women or single out moms for harsh assessment or criticism.

As a matter of fact, the reason I've decided to focus on moms is because of the indispensable role moms play in society. In addition, the strongest human bond is between a mom and her child. We see this intriguing phenomenon even in nature. A child naturally spends more time with her mom than her father, at least during the formative years.

And it's those formative years that really matter. These years are the defining moments of a child. Whatever happens to a child during this period can make or mar her. In fact, this period, as suggested and agreed by different authorities, determines the personality of a person. This is known as the environmental influence.

Traumatic experiences are believed to cause chaos in personality order. Some children respond to terrifying incidents or accidents by developing some traits that are beyond the norm. They become either too defensive or too offensive. Anyway, much will be said on this in a subsequent chapter.

So I've decided to focus on moms because of their invaluable role in parenting and, by extension, society. But there's another science-backed reason I've decided to narrow this topic down to moms, and that's the fact that NPD affects men more than women. Research, which uses U.S. general population samples, finds that the number of men with NPD is almost twice as much as that of women.

This realization prompted me to address NPD among moms, since NPD among women can often be overlooked. I also came to this conclusion when I discovered that the repulsive personality traits described by those who confided in me about their moms share a striking semblance to the traits of NPD. This really cut deep into my heart, and I felt obligated to look into personality disorders and their causes, and I narrowed my search down to NPD, and here we are. End of story.

I'm not saying that NPD is the cause of this abuse, but no one is sure that the problem isn't NPD either. This book has been written to put rest to that confusion and misunderstanding. I'll try to cut and open as many behaviors, habits, and signs in a mom that are smokescreens of NPD as possible.

These behaviors, as we'll see, aren't new behaviors that pop out of the blue. They are behaviors that can be exhibited by anyone. The difference, however, is moderation and sensitivity. When a particular trait is above the line consistently, then there is a personality disorder behind the scenes. It's pertinent that you have this in mind as we consider these signs.

The following are signs that your mom is narcissistic:

She's difficult to placate

We all take offense at something. We all get angry, and our anger might not fizzle out immediately; it could even take days before it evaporates. This doesn't mean we have NPD or any personality disorder. It just means that we're really angry and deeply hurt. But when this lingering anger becomes a normal routine for your mom, then there's something else to it. Could it be NPD? You'll be able to tell as we proceed.

If it always takes your mom time before she lets go of a matter or if she gets easily offended by trivial issues or tries to find fault where none exists, and this happens all the time, then your mom might be struggling with NPD. I truly understand how frustrating this can feel. A mom's love is priceless, but then, an injury inflicted by a mom can be so devastating.

I've seen this insensitivity affect the lives of people I know. Now imagine the many that I don't know. Your mom might have NPD if she's in the habit of not letting an issue go, even when you apologize or make amends. She's just implacable. No water will stop her fire.

The reason she's proving difficult is that she feels challenged by your audacity to offend her in the first place. It doesn't matter that there's no explicit instruction not to do otherwise. Remember, people living with NPD have unrealistic expectations. Suppose you accidentally broke her mirror; she'll feel you did it deliberately to get back at her—because that's what she'd do if she were in your position.

This is because she's reading the entire situation from her own perspective. She's not concerned about your feelings, but only hers. She doesn't want to understand that you didn't break her mirror on purpose and that you're sad that you broke the mirror. In extreme cases of NPD, some moms can go as far as harming their children with broken pieces.

Moms who are in the habit of harming their children are displaying behavior that's not normal. This is the reality. These moms need help from a professional caregiver. And this is why you need to recognize these NPD signs so you will know how best to go about it.

She doesn't want to be questioned or challenged

This is the chief reason people living with NPD find it difficult to keep a job for a long time. They can't keep up with a boss or a colleague who questions or challenges them. And we aren't talking about demanding and cocky bosses who use every opportunity to impress their authority on subordinates.

A person living with NPD will be highly offended when she's questioned. Even if the person who has questioned her point of view does so gently, she'll still be offended. It doesn't matter if the other person is right and she's wrong; she'll feel degraded all the same. As far as she's concerned, she can't go wrong on any issue.

If your mom is always irritated when questioned or challenged intellectually on a point, there's a possibility that she's struggling with NPD. Again, you'll have to consider other traits treated in this book to come to a conclusion. No one is an island of knowledge. So it's okay for your mom to be wrong at times. But if your mom is always claiming to be right, like a greased piglet always escaping from being trapped in error, then a personality disorder is likely the cause.

If she gets really mad at you when you try to let her get your point or shift from her faulty position, and this is almost always the case, I'm convinced that she has a personality disorder, which could be NPD if she also exhibits other traits that are explained in this book.

Like I've stated before, she's insecure and delicate. Your mom may be letting out a roar like a lion on the outside, but deep inside, she's meowing softly. She doesn't want to accept she's wrong or not up to par because she's very poor in handling her own disappointment. This takes us to the next point.

She gets moody after disappointment

Your mom might have NPD if she always feels depressed after a disappointment, especially one that others see as nonissue. There's every reason to be perfectly perfect for people living with NPD. They set unrealistic high expectations for themselves, and when they don't meet them, they feel so bad and become angry.

If you violate any of her written or unwritten rules during this period, you're in for it. She'll make you pay for her misery, even though you're not the direct cause of it. She'll blame you for her disappointment and for her failure. Suppose the proposal she'd expected to be easily approved at work had been unanimously rejected; she'd feel so humiliated. It's normal for everyone to be dejected after rejection, don't get me wrong.

But the person with NPD is more likely to stay depressed without taking care to look at the reason for the dismissal of her proposal. Let's create a scenario to understand this better. Your mom was working on a proposal for her work, and you happened to know a few things about it. You pointed out to her that her job was lousy and that it needed a complete overhaul. But she took offense at you for suggesting her work wasn't up to par. She then defiantly pressed ahead to submit the proposal and the board unanimously rejected it.

This hit her really hard. She doesn't really feel bad about the rejection but for what it means for her pristine reputation. You see, her mind is one exaggerating piece of a biological machine. It sees realities bigger and uglier than they really are. She feels bad that you had been right about the poorly written proposal. She feels bad that another colleague—someone she dislikes and envies, perhaps—had her proposal approved.

The big problem is that she feels she deserves everything. She feels she's always right and others are always wrong. And instead of her going back to ruminate on why things have gone wrong, she'll get depressed and direct her aggression toward you. Note that this can happen to anyone, but a person without NPD will genuinely apologize or look for ways to make amends.

She feels she's entitled to everything

If your mom wants everything to always be about her, to always want to be in the spotlight, even at your peril and discomfort, she's certainly struggling with NPD or another personality disorder, which might be Histrionic Personality Disorder. It may be NPD if she only seeks attention when she feels it'll benefit her.

A mom with NPD can pour cold water on the table if her child is the center of attention. Not even her child is exempted from this competitive and power-grabbing urge. Only one person is entitled to everything, and that has to be her. If your mom often distracts people from shifting attention away from you to herself or to something else, she probably has NPD.

If you're in a warm conversation with someone and your mom feels snubbed, she's likely to be impatient and angry. Why? Because you aren't giving her the special treatment she deserves. You're not allowing her to monopolize the conversation. She can do anything—and she will—

at that moment to kill your joy—even if it means taking a leaf out of the book a person with Histrionic Personality Disorder.

This can be really frustrating for a child, and it can affect her self-esteem. I've promised myself that I won't outrun myself, so I'll save the negative impacts a mom with NPD has on her child for later. But, before then, let me add a few more signs that show your mom is a narcissist.

She's annoyingly patronizing

Does your mom enjoy belittling you and others, while she extols herself? Does she like to put herself on the high table while she puts others on the floor? If the answer is yes, I'm afraid your mom is narcissistic. Nothing sears self-confidence in a child more than a condescending mom! When the mom that's supposed to cushion the effect of a toxic society on her child is the one fueling toxicity, adding salt to injury, it's a very unfortunate and pathetic situation.

You may be doing well at school or in other areas, which is a good thing, but not to a mom with NPD. If your success is getting in the way of your mom, she can belittle your achievement in a moment. If your mom is in the habit of ridiculing or belittling you while making herself appear superior, I can tell you authoritatively that she's narcissistic. Yes, she is!

If she does this, especially when she's not doing well herself, she's definitely narcissistic. Maybe you don't get my point yet, so I'll say it again: those living with NPD don't care about anyone's success—including their children and loved ones—they only care about their success.

It's not normal for your mom to be competitive with you. Don't accept it as normal or listen to anyone who says it is. And it's not okay for your mom to always belittle you in private or in public. She may caution you not to let your success get into your head, but she should not belittle you. She should rejoice with you because your success is her success.

But for a mom struggling with NPD, your success isn't her success. She doesn't see it that way at all. In fact, she sees you as an opponent. Like I said earlier, this isn't normal. She needs help.

She goes gaga when stressed

We can be unsettled when we are stressed. Our smiles can fade away. Our radiance can disappear. We can transfer aggression to someone else. We can look pale, or even break down in tears when things go awry. All this is totally normal, I know.

But it's not normal to go crazy every time we are stressed.

If your mom always misbehaves each time she encounters a problem, she's likely struggling with NPD. It's not normal for your mom to overreact to every discomforting situation she encounters. People living with NPD overreact because of the unnecessary weight they put on themselves.

Their imagined perfection becomes threatened when they encounter a problem they think they can't solve. If a mom living with NPD thinks she competes with other moms, she'll overprotect and overpamper her child, just to prove a point. But if any situation comes up that threatens her sense of superiority, she can be stressed out and maltreat that child.

She's stressed out because she's being a good mom in the first place to impress other moms, not because she sees it as ideal or as a priority. She sees herself in competition with these imaginary or real moms and strives hard to overindulge her child. But other selfish traits of NPD will soon have their toll on her, and she'll give up. This failure on her part to keep being a good mom will stress her. But she'll never own up to the fact that she has failed.

She wants to be praised for nothing

It's a good habit to always be grateful to those who help us. On this premise, there's nothing wrong with being grateful to your mom for the good job she has done. But you might find it inconvenient and even frustrating if your mom always wants you to thank or praise her.

One of the traits of people struggling with NPD is that they have a dramatic sense of self-importance. In other words, they feel they should always be praised, even if they don't do anything that's praiseworthy. So if your mom has NPD, she'll always be fussy when you don't acknowledge her important place in your life.

You may find that she's always probing you to see if you realize her significant role in your life. She's always looking for ways to make you realize that she's done something in your life that no one else could do. Blame this pet peeve of hers on her NPD, which always make her expect others to recognize her indispensable existent and nonexistent achievements.

Even if the achievement is there, it's in her own eyes that it's a big deal. She has an exaggerated sense of everything, remember? And this includes her achievements, even when they are ordinary.

But as far as she's concerned, her toes have to be kissed as an acknowledgment of her achievements.

She's an unbelievable dreamer

If your mom isn't a dreamer, then you can immediately rule out the possibility of her having NPD. This is because dreaming and fantasizing about power, influence, beauty, and dominance is central to why those with NPD behave in the manner they do.

At the center of their behavioral pattern are their distorted life expectations. They go through real struggles in accepting the realities of life. Yes, I've just said the problem. That's where the issue lies. And because of this weakness and rigidity in accepting life, they find it difficult to accept themselves.

They are unable to accept their looks, weaknesses, financial status, family background, and the likes. So they resort to dreaming—where they create their perfect world. This is cool, right? It's not a big deal. After all, we all dream. Well, I'm afraid it's not cool! In fact, it's the biggest deal, and here's why.

It'd have been cool if their dreaming didn't affect their outlook about life and if it didn't affect how they relate to others. It'd have been cool if the hurt and suffering they inflict are just in their dreams.

But they are not. My friends in the real world are hurting and have suffered because of this unrealistic world outlook. Many, as I'm writing this, are going through all kinds of pain.

We all dream. This is very true, but the dreaming of those struggling with NPD is unfortunately merged with reality. This is the challenge. In fact, they live in their Disneyland more than they live in the real world. In their bid to reject reality, they are rejecting sanity. This is why they act in the uncomfortable way they do.

Things might be so bad at home, and a mom struggling with NPD will make a light situation out of it. She'll laugh it off and gives legless assurance that all will be well—even when there's actively nothing she's doing to make things alright. The reason for this is because she's finding comfort in her dreamland, or she's only being whimsical.

If your mom's always like this, then there's every possibility she's living with NPD. If she's in the habit of not reacting to serious issues but always takes trivial issues seriously, then there's a problem.

She wants unalloyed loyalty

Is your mom a general who always wants salutes and no questions? Does she want you to always comply with whatever she says even if it's highly inconvenient for you? Does she want 200 percent loyalty all the time? Then the chances are that she's living with NPD.

People living with NPD don't want anything to alter their expectations, whether they are realistic or not. This is why their decisions are often final. They've said it, they've said. Nothing can be done anymore. The great ones have spoken.

She's thin-skinned

It shouldn't be surprising by now that people living with NPD are thin-skinned. They don't take criticism lightly at all, because doing so will break their bubble and expose their weaknesses. If your mom is struggling with NPD, she'll have big trouble maneuvering her way through criticism.

When she's criticized or feels criticized, expect to see temper tantrums or even tears. At that moment, she can say what she shouldn't say or do what she shouldn't do. This is why people struggling with NPD barely have quality friends because they will always exhibit interpersonal problems that will ruin their friendships.

She's envious of others and skeptical

If your mom always plays down the achievement of other people, she's likely struggling with NPD. While it's true that beauty is in the eye of the beholder, if your mom is always watering down the beauty of others, she might be struggling with narcissism. She may even demean the efforts of her own children.

Her skepticism might be induced by envy. If you were to say a person who treats her like a queen is beautiful, she might obviously agree with you. But the moment the bootlicking stops, she may withdraw her expensive admission of the person's beauty.

She's insensitive and inflexible

If you often find yourself or hear others saying your mom is steely and emotionless, your mom might be struggling with NPD. One of the character traits of those living with NPD is their inflexibility and insensitivity. They find it difficult —I don't want to say they're unable because I strongly believe they can get treatment—to see through the emotions of others.

Their own feelings and needs so becloud people living with NPD that they don't see the negative effects their insensitivity is causing for others.

They are unwilling to recognize the needs of those around them.

Causes of Narcissistic Personality Disorder

The law of cause and effect states that there is a cause for every effect and every effect has a cause. That is, every action has a reaction. There is a cause for every action. In other words, nothing happens by chance. This is quite interesting. If we apply this eternal law to our discourse, we'll see that NPD has a cause and effect.

Situations and things are the way they are because of direct or indirect causes and actions. Things don't just happen. We can also learn from Newton's law of motion. Newton's first law of motion states that an object will remain at rest unless an external force acts on it. Similarly, an object will remain in a state of motion unless an external force acts on it.

If we apply Newton's law here, it suggests that NPD isn't going to be in operation if something hasn't set it loose in the first place. In this chapter, we'll be looking at the external force or forces that bring NPD into existence.

But before we proceed, I must admit that there's no consensus among scholars as to what causes NPD. The reason for disagreement and various postulations is because NPD, like other personality disorders, is purely psychological. There are no physical signs on the body. You don't just look at a person and say, "Oh, that guy has NPD."

However, many, including myself, agree that genetics and the environment have a lot to do with the etiology of NPD. Modern researchers also agree that NPD is a result of genetic makeup and environmental influence. I'll explain these causes one after the other.

Genetics

There's every reason to want to link genetic development with NPD. This is because everything begins in the gene: from physical appearance to personality traits. Genes determine our hair color, eye color, skin color, height, etc. Genes, as units of heredity, are how progenitors transfer their qualities to their offspring.

We all have two copies of each gene, one from the father and one from the mother. I'll quickly run you through the basics of genetics so that you can understand the place of genetics in NPD. Don't worry; I'll make it as simple as possible. Trust me.

Obviously, it's not all traits that are transferred from the parents to children—this explains why everyone has unique features. If there were no differences whatsoever, everyone would look the same way and behave the same way. Wouldn't that be scary! But thanks to some differences, though small, in our genes, we are all unique.

So, how is genetics a cause of NPD? If one of the parents has NPD, is it possible for the child to inherit it? That's a one-million-dollar question. Before I answer it, I must briefly explain why genetic disorders occur in the first place. Disorders occur in the gene because of mutation.

Gene mutation is the permanent alteration in a gene. This alteration is a complete accidental change from the usual traits of a gene. Mutation can be hereditary and nonhereditary. Our focus is on hereditary mutation. For instance, a person suffering from sickle cell anemia has received two mutated genes from both parents. One mutated gene can't cause sickle cell anemia.

Also, a person is an albino because he has received two defective melanin genes from both parents. Albinism can't occur without gene donations from both parents. Sickle cell anemia and albinism are both examples of autosomal recessive inheritance, in which two mutated genes are required.

However, in autosomal dominant inheritance, only one copy of a mutant gene is passed down to a child.

The question then is: Is NPD an autosomal dominant inheritance or an autosomal recessive inheritance? If we say it's autosomal dominant recessive, we're saying the mutant NPD gene is passed down from only a parent. And if we say it's an autosomal recessive gene, we are saying the mutant NPD gene is passed down from both the mother and the father.

But we've got a problem on our hands: there's nothing called an NPD gene that makes someone develop unhealthy narcissistic traits, just as there's no "good-mom" gene that makes someone a good mom or "good-grade" gene that gives someone good grade. If genetics has a part to play in NPD at all, it would be a product of several defective genes working together.

I believe you now see the reason there's an argument about the role of genetics in NPD? The whole thing is complex. There's no straightforward answer. I decided to give you the basics of genetics so that you'll understand why there's perplexity in the scholastic world about NPD and other personality disorders and the role genes play in their cause.

The obvious conclusion then is: though research and genetic studies show that genetics play a role in NPD development, the exact way it does that is still a mystery. No one actually knows. Maybe in the future, with more advanced science and technology, the clear role genetics play will be discovered. But for now, no one is sure.

Environmental Factors

Unlike the genetic factor, it's clear how environmental factors cause NPD. Environmental factors are external factors that influence a person's behavior. I'd like to explain the place of the environment in our lives briefly. This will help me to lay the groundwork for the environmental factors that cause NPD. I'll break it down in a very simple way.

You see, while genes make us who we are, the environment shapes up who we are. That is, the environment is the medium through which our genes express themselves. Genes determine your hair, color, height, intelligence, and even health, but the environment can cause slight or major modifications.

This means that a person who's fair in complexion can become darker under continued exposure to sunlight. Did you just say "tanning!" What happens when you tan is that you're allowing the sunlight, an external influence, to make some modifications to the genes in your melanin.

What I'm trying to say is that the genetic instructions that we are born with can be rewritten over time by environmental factors. Our genes can be enhanced or impaired as life happens. So, the similar genetic makeup of identical twins can be altered based on environmental factors. This is why even identical twins with similar genetic have different personalities.

Animal species of the same kind may end up with different skin colors and structures because of the different habitats they find themselves in. An example is the difference in fur color of polar bears and brown bears. Same animal, different environment, different look. It's the same with human folks too.

These environmental factors affect how genes express themselves. For example, some drugs and chemicals can affect the genetic development of a fetus. These chemicals are called teratogens. It's not like babies born with birth defects don't have a normal embryonic formation. Some drugs are harmless to adults but extremely dangerous to embryos. They can alter the genetic codes and cause terrible mutations. This is why pregnant women are cautioned against using any drugs.

I'll like to stop here now that you get the basics. All I'm trying to let you know is that environmental factors play a very significant role in the cause of NPD. We don't know the extent to which genetics induce NPD, but we do know how environmental factors, interpersonal interaction, especially, cause NPD. It's these environmental factors I'll be addressing now. I'll group the causes under two categories: childhood experiences and psychological factors.

Childhood Experiences

Recent studies support the notion that parenting plays a great role in NPD development. How a child is raised to a large extent, can negatively shape her behavior. The home is the first place of learning. It's a place of nurture and grooming for the future, so its influence on a child can't be overlooked.

The mother-child relationship is crucial, especially at the early stage of childhood. The mental health of those involved determines the health of any relationship. This is very much applicable to parenting. The health of the relationship between mother and child will affect the mental health of the child.

Children have powerful memories and delicate minds. Parents should, therefore, be very careful about what they do, words they say, and their body language in fr0nt of their little ones.

I'll now be addressing parental behaviors that can encourage NPD in a child.

Overindulgence

This may baffle you—and I'm not surprised. I mean, how could excessive indulgence lead to a child developing unhealthy narcissism? Recent studies have shown a link between overindulgence and narcissism. Children who are overpampered have a higher chance of growing up with NPD than those who receive moderate care.

Parents who overpamper their children do so out of love. They think they are doing their children good. But the opposite is true. What they are actually doing is causing them harm. Overpampered children are at higher risk of having their egos pumped beyond measure.

Don't get me wrong; a healthy dose of pampering is certainly good for a child. It's good for mothers to pay attention to a child's needs and meet her requests. It's good to lavish your love on your child and make her feel like the princess she is in your kingdom. In fact, children who are appropriately nurtured have good self-esteem and healthy mental health.

But it's not a good thing, nor has ever been, for parents to overindulge their children. Mothers who always go overboard to meet the requests and wants of their children are planting seeds of narcissism in them. Notice that I use "wants," not needs. We should do all we can to meet the genuine needs of our children, but we must learn to say "No" to frivolous wants and requests that aren't beneficial to our sweet little ones.

When you grant all that your child wants, and you go on a gratification spree to fill the never-stopping growling desires of your child's stomach, you're conveying a wrong message to her. You're telling her that, "It's okay always to crave what you desire, and it's okay always to get what you want, even if you've got to whine and cry and throw things to get them."

A bit of over pampering, a bit of perennial gratification, and a bit excessive indulgence all serve as a fertile ground for narcissism to grow. Every child and everyone has a narcissistic tendency, as you'll later see in this book but it's also why parents need to be very careful in how they raise their kids.

The seeds of narcissism are in every child, that's for sure. But overindulgence is what makes the difference, what makes a child become a narcissist later in life.

Negligence

"Since overindulgence is harmful to a child's mental health, shouldn't parents withdraw their care altogether?" you may want to ask. Well, that would be equally risky for the child's mental well-being. Excessive care is as dangerous as a lack of care. A child who receives excessive care and a child who lacks care are both at equal risk of developing NPD. How so? Good question!

Recall that I said every child is narcissistic, as it's our human genetic makeup. We all have narcissistic traits, and it's okay if it's a healthy dose. A child who lacks care may develop narcissism as a means of survival. I'll create a story to help you get this important point.

A single mom has two children, Mary and Jessy. She loves the younger child Jessy more than Mary, and she always shows it at every opportunity. She spends almost all the time with Jessy, listening to her complaints, wants needs, and idiosyncrasies. Whatever Jessy points to, she gets, even if her object of desire is in Mary's possession. As a result,

Jessy feels she's more special than her sister. She feels she's entitled to everything.

On the other hand, Mary feels awful and sad. It hurts her that her mom prefers her sister to her. In fact, she has thought so many times that her mom isn't her biological mother. She feels empty on the inside. She feels like an outsider. She feels bad that Jessy gets all she wants while she barely gets all she needs. "Life is cruel," she often says.

In response to her hostile environment, Mary builds a fantasy world where she's the favorite child—except that in this imaginary world, her mom isn't there. She replaces her with her favorite celebrity. In that world of magic and butterflies, she's not only the favorite girl, but she's the only child. Well, Jessy is also in that world, but she's just her maid.

I hope you enjoyed that story! Joking apart, you get the point of the story. Both children develop narcissism in different environments. So narcissism is both a xerophyte, that can grow and survive in a desert (hostile environment), and a hydrophyte, that can grow and survive in water (friendly environment).

So, parents, especially moms, have to be balanced in raising their children. Too much care should be avoided, and too little care shouldn't be on the table. It's like sugar in the bloodstream—high sugar levels are harmful, and low sugar levels are equally harmful. Don't be afraid to deny your child's wants. It's okay to let your child know that she can't always get what she wants, because in life we don't always get what we want.

In fact, it's good to deliberately reject a child's want so that you can teach her this vital life lesson. Even if you can comfortably get her that thing she wants—and even if you'll give it to her later—it's a good idea to refrain from giving it to her once in a while. This will make your child live in reality and know that it's okay not to get everything.

You'll also have to carry your partner, family members, and friends along. Though you may not overindulge your child, if your partner, family members, or friends constantly do, it's still risky.

Negligence is a terrible thing to do to a child. At that formative age, what a child needs are tender love, attention, and companionship. It's your duty as a parent to provide these—more than that, it's your duty not to overdo it.

Parental Manipulative Behavior

Children see everything their parents do, and they learn from them directly and indirectly.

Manipulative parents are passing down the wrong message and influence on their children. If a relative or a friend or anyone at all is in the habit of taking you on guilt trips, blaming you and never accepting blame, treating you condescendingly and deflating your balloon of confidence; that person is manipulative.

Take, for example, a mom who takes pleasure in manipulating others to have her way is teaching her child the art of manipulation. Such a child may grow up manipulating people. A manipulative mom will intentionally use your weakness to exp0loit you, to undermine your confidence and make you feel bad. She'll always attempt to paint your ugly version to the outside world. This action may prompt the child to seek solace in a fantasy world.

Both the act of manipulation and the effects of manipulation on a child can both cause a child to be narcissistic. In other words, a child can learn the manipulative behavior of her mom and become narcissistic, or the terrible effects of her manipulative mom can push her toward narcissism, or it can be a combination of both.

Manipulative people are so annoying and frustrating. If you've come across one before, you'll agree with me totally, you can never win against them in an argument, not because they are always right, but because they are always going to stick with their point. They will always want to control you, wanting you to do what they want. And they won't care about your opinion.

Your emotions are like a ping pong ball to them, which they can play with as they please. If being heartless is what will make them be in charge, then they will be heartless. They are in it for anything that will make them be in charge and don't care about your mental wellbeing.

A manipulative mom will always blame you or others for her woes. She'll never accept her role in her problems. If, for instance, you tell her of your desire to go for a vacation with your uncle, and she doesn't want you to go, she may say, "I work day and night just to make you comfortable, so is this how you'll repay me? You want to leave me alone, just like that?" It's just one scenario out of many. I hope you get the point.

This puerile and cruel art can guilt-trip you and make you feel bad. Apart from canceling your trip, you may also believe you're heartless and ungrateful. You have done what she wants you to do without her having to say it outright. Mission accomplished! This practice is called "gaslighting." I'll explain this properly in the next chapter.

Exaggerated Assessment

There's nothing wrong with assessing something and giving a verdict. It's well within your right to criticize or praise someone or something. Your evaluation is your right. However, evaluation that goes overboard isn't good. Exaggerated assessment can be in the form of excessive criticism or hypercriticism and excessive praise or overpraise.

Hypercriticism

Parents who always over-criticize their children may end up instilling fear and self-doubt in them. A child who is always over-criticized for her wrongdoing may lose confidence in herself and may become paranoid. She may be skeptical of genuine praise and rebuff sincere criticism. She may also find it pretty difficult to give compliments and appreciate others.

To maneuver her way around her parent's criticism, she may have to turn a deaf ear to criticism altogether, and in so doing, she may become arrogant and insensitive to external evaluations. This defensive technique may encourage narcissism.

I've not suggested in any way that children shouldn't be criticized or corrected for their wrongdoing. Of course, they should. I've only said they shouldn't be over-criticized; in the same way, no one should be over-criticized. Hypercriticism is excessive criticism that's unfair and disproportionate to the wrong committed.

If hypercriticism could be unsettling for an adult, think about how unsettling it could be for a child. That's my point.

Overpraise

Now I'm not saying you should shun criticism and go for excessive praise. Both are two sides of the same coin. Both are extremes. Just as you shouldn't over-criticize, you shouldn't also overpraise, which is an excessive commendation that's way beyond the good done.

Excessive praise isn't good for anyone, least of all children. Praises that are over the top can get into the head of a child. She may begin to feel that she's so intelligent and special than her sibling and other children. It's not hard to figure out how too much praise can reduce productivity.

A child that always receives excessive praise won't see the need to improve herself or work harder. She'll simply assume she's doing great already. I know parents who overpraise their children mean well, but they aren't doing well. This is the plain truth. There are other ways you can motivate a child to keep doing well rather than just praising her all the time. Nobody enjoys perennially receiving criticisms, but then receiving excessive praise isn't beneficial either.

Praise is excessive if it's given at the wrong time, to the wrong person, or with the wrong motive. If all the time you go about praising your child for things she ought to do, it will give her a sense of entitlement. Anytime she doesn't get it, she will feel sad. Suppose you always give your child chocolate for doing a chore; she may lose interest in that chore if she doesn't get her chocolate. This is because she's come to feel entitled to the privilege that comes with that chore. Remember, one of the behavioral traits of a narcissist is a sense of entitlement.

But just when is praise too much? I recommend what I call the "do-and-commend" rule. That is, don't praise your child for no reason. Let your praise be based on reality. Let your commendation have a target—I mean reasonable targets. It's good to commend on your child's good looks, but don't make a music out of it. And don't compare her with other children, because doing so may make her feel superior.

And also, don't praise your child for doing what she ought to do. This way, you'll be teaching your child the importance of hard work. You should definitely commend your child's ability and encourage her to keep it up, but don't overdo it, or slight other children in her presence.

The whole point is that your criticism or commendation should be commensurate with your assessment. There's a risk of your child developing narcissism.

Psychological Factors

The cause of NPD can also be mental and emotional. That is, it's not what a child sees her parents or others do, but what is done to her. Some life experiences can be so harrowing and agonizing for the delicate mind of a child to bear. And to maintain some sanity, the child will either be offensive or defensive.

These defensive or offensive measures are the child's way of coping and responding to the trauma of the abuse. There's no gainsaying about the evil of abuse in our world; instead, it's a cruel reality, which has caused untold pain and distress to many children.

Children can be traumatized by what they see or what they experience, and what their innocent minds see or go through. Sexual abuse, verbal abuse, parental substance dependence, death, violence, and parents not living together or divorced can all contribute to NPD development, and I'll briefly explain them one after the other.

Sexual Abuse

Sexual abuse isn't only when any form of sexual act is done with the child, but also any form of sexual activity that's done in the presence of a child. Sexual abuse can have long-lasting damaging effect on the poor child. Exposing a child to pornographic materials, masturbating in the presence of a child, chatting or texting a child about sex implicitly or explicitly, sex trafficking (sexual slavery), standing nude before a child are all forms of sexual abuse.

Any of these acts is like a sudden introduction of a virus into a child's mind. A child that's sexually abused may become confused, frightened, uncertain, paranoid, and even dangerous to self and others. She may resort to harming herself or her violator. She may begin to be overprotective or keep to herself completely. She may even come to hate the opposite sex or sex itself. Sexual abuse can lead to many things, including NPD.

Verbal Abuse

A child who is always called names, wrongly accused, reproached, snubbed, cussed, screamed at, humiliated with unkind words, belittled with demeaning words, criticized for nothing or nonissue or over-criticized for a genuine issue is being verbally abused.

Words employed in the verbal assault are always assorted with anger and hatred. They are fueled by bitterness. This is one way to know if you're being verbally abused. Parents who always yell at their children are abusing them. When a child can't say or do anything without being yelled at and criticized, it's going to have a toll on her mental health.

Parental Substance Dependability

Parents who are given to excessive drug use and alcohol consumption will find it difficult to cater to the physical and mental needs of their children. And let's be very clear about this—and you may find out yourself—parental neglect is a legit form of child abuse on its own. Yeah, that's pretty correct.

Parental neglect becomes inevitable when parents are addicted to drugs or alcohol because a parent can't be in the right frame of mind to attend to her child's needs if she can't gratify her alcohol or drug dependence. It's only after she's satisfied her own needs that she may attend to the need of her child. The lack of physical and emotional care and attention can lead to NPD in a child.

Death of Loved Ones

We all respond to grief in different ways. Some people, even adults, never pull themselves together after the death of a loved one. Some children, because they depend on their parents, especially their moms, find it extremely difficult to cope with the loss. This also extends to the death of a sibling, caregiver or anyone close to the child emotionally and physically.

And such can be really distressing for a child who doesn't get adequate support. Such a child may withdraw into an imaginary world—where there's nothing like death or grief—where she sees her late mom or dad.

Parents not Living Together or Divorced

Many couples on the brink of short-term separation or divorce dither because of the negative impact such a move might have on their children. It's a good thing that many consider the mental health of their children. Break up certainly affects children. They can become angry, sad, and embittered at one or both parents.

They may isolate themselves and misbehave in protest of the separation. They may feel abandoned by the parent who is away or feel isolated by the one who is around. In any case, separation could have a negative influence on the overall mental development of a child.

Violence

Conflicts between parents surely do affect a child. If dad and mom are always arguing and yelling at each other, the child will be affected. The child may feel guilty, thinking she's the cause. She may feel disturbed and confused if the altercation is escalating. All this can make her keep to herself.

A child who has seen the horrors of war or any physical violence may be traumatized for the short or long term. She may become hardened and emotionless by them. This can make her be insensitive to the needs of others, thereby becoming narcissistic.

Now that we've treated the various causes of NPD, it's time for us to treat the impact a narcissistic mom has on her daughter. I wanted you to understand what NPD is and its causes before I addressed this important issue.

Chapter Summary

The behaviors of those living with NPD are normal behaviors exhibited by humans but can be seen as going overboard to a certain extent. Everyone is narcissistic to some extent; everyone has high self-esteem; everyone has a sense of self-importance. However, those with NPD exhibit an exaggerated form of these traits consistently. This is why it's called a disorder.

Based on firsthand information from those who have been abused by their parents in their childhood and even in adulthood, and from my sound knowledge about NPD; I can tell you that your mom is inappropriately narcissistic (yes, there's a dose of narcissism that's healthy. I'll come to that later), if she's selfish, pretentious, patronizing, insensitive to feelings, belittle or resent the achievements of others.

It's a fact that those living with NPD can be annoying and dangerous. Interestingly, and not so surprising, they may not even realize that they need the help of a professional, and those around them may also not know the underlying problem behind their erratic behavior. So the situation is frustrating for all. In the next chapter, we'll be looking at the causes of NPD.

CHAPTER TWO

THE EFFECTS OF BEING RAISED BY A NARCISSISTIC MOM

You need to see the agony and pain with which those who confided in me still retell their mothers' words and actions. This is even though their terrible maternal experiences happened years ago. Though it was years ago, the pain is still alive and real. The bitterness won't just go away.

Words are powerful—they can heal or injure, make or mar—but even more so if they are the words of a mother. Hearing terrible words from your mother consistently is a terrible experience. The extent and severity of pain depend on the one who inflicts it. Though abuse is painful enough on its own, it's even more painful and has a long-lasting effect on a child if it comes from their mother.

Verbal abuse, physical abuse, and other forms of abuse by a mother can all have psychological effects on a child. The child can develop anxiety, depression, low self-esteem, paranoia, etc. I'll address some of these effects now.

Oversensitivity or Insensitivity

Children who are raised by a narcissist tend to be oversensitive or aren't sensitive at all, and you can't blame them. They unconsciously learned to read their mom's emotions and body language when they were growing up. But the problem is, narcissistic moms are difficult to read and don't have emotions.

So, to survive under the parentage of a narcissistic mom, they had to become more sensitive to the mixed signals they received from their moms. Narcissistic moms are many things, but being straightforward and consistent isn't one of them. Anything that will make them stay in charge and dominate is what they will do. They are highly demanding and critically manipulative.

A manipulative mom is like software updates that a child will have to constantly update her operating system to function well under her tutelage and care. This experience can be really frustrating for a child. The child will always have to be on the watch out to see how to position herself for the next assault better. The child may develop a thick skin or a thin skin in response to her insatiable mom.

None of the two response is good. A thick skin will help the child be insensitive to emotions and evaluation, and thin skin will make her too sensitive to emotions and evaluation. This weakness can be exploited by those she's in a relationship with. Her excessively empathetic nature can be taken advantage of by her friends to manipulate her. And for an insensitive person, she'll miss out on many things.

Children who are raised by a narcissistic mom may end up having a problem with sensitivity. It's either they are too sensitive or not sensitive at all. This will no doubt affect their relationships. They will have a problem dealing with people's words and actions.

Insecurity

When you doubt yourself, you don't have confidence in your ability, or you feel ashamed of your looks, then you're insecure. Children raised by narcissists, especially girls, are always in doubt about their looks. They've heard "You're so ugly" and "There's nothing good in you" and "Have you seen your horrible-looking self in the mirror lately?" and other verbal assaults countless times.

They've been compared with every bad thing, such as a rotten egg, and they've come to believe it. You can't blame them—you'll agree with me that mom's words, and indeed words of those who are dear to us, have the uncanny ability to cut our hearts more deeply than those of outsiders. I think the words of our loved ones are designed to affect us profoundly so that they can soothe our wearied hearts. Unfortunately, however, this verbal power has always been abused.

Children who are raised by narcissistic moms find it difficult to believe they are capable of doing almost anything. This negative seed of insecurity has devastating effects on children—even well into their adult lives. I know this because I've seen it in 100 percent of the women who've confided in me about their narcissistic moms.

I remember how one of my friends doubted her ability when I asked her to do something. Even though she could do this task effortlessly, she still doubted her ability. In the end, she did a very good job. You should have been there to see how phenomenal her joy was when I commended her work. That's what she'd not been getting from her mom.

This woman is in her forties, yet the impact of her narcissistic mom was still very much at work. Another thing I've come to realize is that this insecurity affected her relationships. I can confidently tell you that 80 percent of women who have confided in me about their narcissistic moms have problems with their first husbands. Some have remarried, and some haven't.

Now please, don't get me wrong. I'm not in any way judging them or suggesting that the divorce was their fault. As a matter of fact, I'm saying it's not their fault. I deduced two things from their stories:

1. Their partners exploited their insecurity and sensitivity;

2. Their partners weren't lenient with their lack of confidence and sensitivity.

Insecure people are anxious, give in to self-pity, timid, and skeptical. All of these will work against them in all their relationships. Do you know the biggest reason why those raised by narcissistic moms may be insecure? Because they will be seeing the image of their moms in others.

They've lived with poor self-esteem with their moms all their lives, especially in their formative years. It's going to be very difficult to have self-pride when dealing with others because they have come to have a poor perception of themselves from barrages of humiliation and embarrassment.

Skeptical or Gullible

A person that's raised by a narcissistic mom may have an irrational distrust of others or may be easily deceived and exploited. Neither of these is a healthy spice for relationship breakfast. While growing up under the unenviable guidance of a narcissistic mom, she's had her feelings toyed with and her emotional needs unmet.

For a person that's heard that she's the most terrible and dumbest person that ever lived, you wouldn't blame her if she doesn't believe it when someone tells her she's very beautiful or very smart. People who are raised by narcissistic moms are often skeptical of commendation and too-good-to-be-true words.

In fact, in rare cases, they may find commendation and appreciative statements offensive, because they assume they are being deceived or manipulated. This attitude will surely affect their relationships. This kind of person doesn't accept praise. Do you blame them? This is only one side of the coin, however.

The other side of the coin is those who actually crave recognition and welcome appreciative gestures. Remember, we're all different. How we respond to situations differs. Two children might be raised by a narcissistic mom and end up behaving differently. One may be very skeptical of people's commendation, and the other may actually crave it. But neither positions are good.

Many children who have been raised by narcissistic moms need validation to feel good. The fact is, in their childhoods they were denied motherly care and attention. They may even have been called names. These were children who expected love from their mom, but were never shown it. They were disapproved of and brought up to believe that they were lacking in some way, hence requiring validation from the people around them when they were adults.

Their mothers did not fulfill their hopes of being loved. The problem with this scenario is that they grow up needing validation even more than would be normally expected, but will still feel that mom's opinion matters and will continue to experience her ire and disapproval, even when they are adults.

Poor Social Relations

Since the horrible effects of narcissism are inflicted during the mother-child relationship, it's not surprising that children who are raised by narcissistic moms have poor social skills. The home is a place of knowledge, and the mother is the first teacher of a child. So it's very natural for the child to pick some selfish character traits that will later affect his social relationships with others.

Such a child may unknowingly be too demanding, oversensitive, patronizing, insensitive, etc. in her dealings with others. Actions, they say, speak louder than words. This is very true when it comes to character development. But even if someone somehow escapes imbibing some narcissistic traits of a narcissistic mom, she may not be able to escape her distorted perception of others. She may be too reserved in relationships, mostly keeping to herself. She may not be good at initiating a conversation or keeping one going. These are relationship spoilers.

It's unfortunate that many grown children of narcissistic moms are still living in the shadows of themselves, even though they live far away from their moms. They haven't found the help they need—that's for those who realize they need help, because many still don't know they need help.

Interestingly, all those who confided in me are far from their moms—some as far as living on different continents. But it isn't just enough to keep a narcissistic mom at a distance. Don't get me wrong. I recommend keeping a distance, as you'll see in the last part of this book, but all I'm saying is that keeping a distance while your mind is still close to your past, isn't effective.

Your past isn't complete without your narcissistic mom. You know that as well as I do. So it's futile to just keep your mom at arm's length without taking further proactive steps. Until you address the root of this matter, which I'll discuss later, you may find yourself suffering from isolation and depression.

Post-Traumatic Stress Disorder (PTSD)

We handle circumstances differently. While some can recover from the horrible experience they went through in the hand of their narcissistic moms, some aren't able to fully recover. The traumas they've been through keep playing out in their minds, and whenever this happens, they go crazy.

Anything can trigger those ugly childhood memories, leading to the transfer of aggression on loved ones, such as a partner, a child, a friend, a colleague, or even a stranger. The triggered person may find that she's yelling or saying hurtful words to others out of agony and bitterness. This will, in turn, affect their relationships.

Such a person may end up hating the word "mother" or even hating all mothers, or even all women. This mental state needs immediate attention. Such a person should seek professional help. Those who have PTSD try to live in denial of reality to cope, but this method solves nothing—besides, it's risky. Triggers will always come. How many people will know their taboos, what to say, and not to say? The best thing is to face their fears once and for all. It's not easy, I know. It's a big step, but you've got to take that big leap!

Parenting Styles between Mom and Daughter

As the title indicates, my focus is on relationships between a mother and a child. But the techniques are also beneficial for a mother-son relationship, a father-daughter relationship, and a father-son relationship. Every daughter wants to have a fantastic relationship with her mom. And I've yet to see a mom who doesn't want a beautiful relationship with her daughter.

Unfortunately, it's easier said or wished for than done. After all, if wishes were horses, beggars would ride. Human relationships, generally, can be very complex, family relationships especially. The reason any relationship is complex is that two individuals are involved. An individual is a distinctive person with her desires, reasoning, outlook, and idiosyncrasies.

Relationships are never a one-person thing. They are made up of at least two individuals with different reasoning, likes, dislikes, appeals, desires, and expectations. This, my dear reader, is the major reason relationships are complex. Yes, they are complex, but they aren't unmanageable. And it's not like there're no wonderful relationships, anyway.

Don't be deceived, though. I know many mother-daughter relationships are already damaged beyond repair as I write, and many more are on the brink of dissolution, but there are still as many good mother-daughter relationships. Now, this doesn't mean that these people have perfect relationships because no relationship is perfect.

In other words, we all have our flaws, weaknesses, and shortcomings, but how we manage them is what makes the difference. There are steps to take to have a wonderful mother-daughter relationship. These steps are also applicable to other relationships. In order not to be presumptuous, let me say that these steps are best taken during childhood. So they may not be effective for mother-daughter relationships that are damaged already though they may salvage those currently drifting on stormy seas. I'll be addressing them one after the other.

Responsibility

If individuals in any relationship play their parts and do what's expected of them, life will be good. In a mother-child relationship, both the mother and the child have roles to play. Think of a relationship as two people carrying a load. If one person isn't handling her side well, the other person will bear the pressure and burden and will stress out with time.

The ideal style of parenting should involve both the mother and the child doing their duty fervently. The mother must cater to the physical and emotional needs of her daughter. She shouldn't neglect her child's needs. But it's also not her duty to overindulge her daughter. As I've shown earlier, overindulgence is an irresponsible act any mother is capable of doing to a child. That's quite frank, but it's quite true.

A responsible mother pays attention to her girl and listens to her. She meets her needs and teaches her vital lessons of life. It's the responsibility of the daughter to obey her mother and carry her along in her actions. Mother-daughter relationship will be easier to manage if those involved carry out their duties.

Healthy Boundaries and Mutual Respect

Mother and child should respect each other's boundaries. What's acceptable and what's not should be defined. This is very important. The mother should know that her girl is an individual, even though she gave birth to her, and the daughter should know that she needs to respect the individuality of her mom.

Mutual respect is essential in a mother-daughter relationship, as it is in every relationship. Conflicts will be at a low point if mother and daughter respect each other's boundaries. The mother shouldn't barge into her daughter's room if she doesn't like it, and the daughter shouldn't sneak out without telling her mom. The child will feel confident that her mom respects her space, and the mother will be happy that her daughter respects her instructions.

The idea of setting boundaries will help the self-esteem of those involved and help keep the bond stronger. Setting boundaries will also help mother and daughter know each other better, and won't give room for provocative assumptions.

Flexibility and Compromise

Every healthy relationship involves individuals who are willing to compromise. If the mother isn't willing to compromise, there will be problems. No one knows it all, not even a mother. The mother shouldn't always want to have her way. She should intentionally cave into the child once in a while; this way she'll be helping her daughter build her confidence.

Instead of the mother always denying her child's requests outright, she should learn to let her daughter see genuine reasons why she denies her requests. It may be that the timing isn't right or the wherewithal to grant the request isn't available. Then, the mother should allow her daughter to respond.

But if you see that you should grant her requests based on her responses, you should be willing to grant her that request. Engaging your daughter in a conversation this way will make the bond stronger. The daughter shouldn't always want to have her own way either. She must learn to be flexible and make do with the present situation. This is how healthy relationships are maintained. Humility is key.

Accept Differences

For a mother-child relationship to thrive, mother and daughter must know that no two individuals are the same—not even identical twins. Mothers should know and appreciate that their daughters are different from them. No matter the resemblance between a mother and a daughter, they are still two individuals who inevitably have their differences.

Even the similarities outnumber the differences; those few differences could cause long-lasting damage. It can be hard for some mothers to accept that their daughters don't share the same passions they have for something and the same for daughters. Differences are bound to happen because our feelings, understandings, and reasoning vary.

We don't have the same eyes, so we see the world differently. The sooner we understand this, the better our relationships will be. These differences are more obvious in relationships between mothers and adult daughters because we learn to know ourselves better as we grow.

Mothers and daughters need to accept and respect their differences. This is how their relationship can last. If you check every damaged mother-daughter relationship, failure to accept each other's differences is a contributing factor.

Approachable

One of the reasons for a strained mother-child relationship is unapproachability. If the mother is up there and isn't easy to relate to, that relationship is compromised. The mother should be approachable and available for her daughter, especially during childhood. This is extremely essential.

Unfortunately, this is where many mothers miss the point. They only realize it when it's too late. I know a person, let's call her Andrea, who can't relate well with her mother. Andrea was always sad to go home during breaks while in college. She couldn't wait to graduate and be forever free from her mom. Andrea is embittered because her mom didn't call her unless she called first, didn't have time for her, and didn't meet her needs. And that's how her mom has been since childhood.

Now that Andrea is married, her mom is trying to get along with her. She confided in me that she wished she could get along with her mom, but it's so awkward for her. It's an experience she's not used to. And I don't blame her.

Many mother-daughter relationships are like that of Andrea and her mom. The daughters are so used to a life without their moms that having them in their lives now feels somehow awkward and unnatural. To avoid this, mothers should be approachable and friendly. There's a place for discipline, and there's a way for friendship.

Self-Control

We all need to exercise self-control because we are all individuals with distinctive selves. We need self-control because we are emotional and rational beings. This means that we have emotions and we make decisions. Since we make decisions all the time, it's very important to have control over our emotions, so that we won't make the wrong decisions in the heat of the moment.

Mothers and daughters need to exercise self-control at all times in their relationships. They must learn to control their emotions in order not to say terrible words or act inappropriately. Words are verbal weapons of mass destruction: they can destroy a relationship forever.

Self-control is the ability to discipline yourself from spitting out appalling words you mean or don't mean and refraining from undertaking actions you'll regret later. Lack of self-control has ground many relationships to a halt. It's an issue that shouldn't be taken for granted.

Gaslighting and its Effects on Adult Children

It's good to be concerned about children who are raised by narcissistic moms. As I've shown, the experience is terrible, and my heart goes out to these children. But equally more heartbreaking is the prolific number of adults who are still going through the pain of being raised by narcissistic moms.

This is why, before I round up this chapter, I've decided to explain the effects of gaslighting on adult children. Proper understanding of the impacts of this narcissistic abuse on adults will help us have a better understanding of the ordeal children with narcissistic moms go through.

Gaslighting is the act of psychologically manipulating someone into doubting their own sanity or reality, leading them to think they are the one who's at fault or they are the problem. Gaslighting is one of the weapons of people with NPD. Narcissistic moms subject their child to emotional abuse by gaslighting them into thinking they are the problem.

The danger of gaslighting is that it makes its victims mix reality and imagination up. A mom who continually blames her child for her woes and for everything will manipulate the child to come to see herself as the problem. As a consequence, the child will grow up believing she's the problem. She may always apologize, even when there's no need to; she may feel she's said something she shouldn't have said; she may even make excuses for those who wrong her because she's been used to being the bad egg. She's been manipulated so much that she's lost her confidence in herself. Since she questions her own sanity, she will find it tough to make decisions on her own without asking for input from those close to her.

One thing I noticed among those who confided in me—and though they may not be aware of it—is that they often want me to validate their decisions. They are always happy when I tell them their decisions are cool. I am lead to believe they lack the confidence to make decisions on their own. I say this because it's a pattern I've seen in our conversations.

Mental manipulation is an emotional roller coaster, and its impacts can be devastating. Those who had been gaslighted for a considerable length of time are at higher risk of falling victim to gas lighters again. They can be gaslighted by their partners, bosses, colleagues, or even friends. Anyone who knows you enough can gaslight you.

A narcissistic mom, of course, knows her child best. She knows areas her child is vulnerable in and areas where she's strong. But her focus will be on the child's vulnerabilities. She may tell the child her feelings are wrong, and she shouldn't be feeling that way. She may guilt-trip the child into thinking her action is an act of betrayal. She may set the child against her dad or sibling because narcissists are powerful where there's division.

In short, she'll do anything to make the child a zombie. She aims to frustrate the child until she goes crazy and loses the strength to think or protest so that she'll do anything her mom says without thinking. When this happens, the child's volition has been broken, and it'll take professional care and intentional personal efforts to have it fixed.

Many people are living with a damaged volition. They've lost the fight long ago to their narcissistic moms. This is why they are easily threatened even by their partners and children, who've come to know their weakness. It's easy for narcissists to gaslight because they don't care about how the feelings of others. All they care about is their self-importance, dominance, and survival, and they will do anything to keep it that way, even if it means gaslighting their loved ones.

Chapter Summary

The pain of narcissistic abuse is real, and its effects are affecting people all around us more than we realize. Narcissistic moms are around us, abusing their children in all sorts of terrible ways. The sad part is that children who are being raised by narcissistic moms grow up feeling unfulfilled and empty. They feel insecure and stupid. And some even grow up to be mean.

This isn't the ideal way of parenting. A mother-child relationship should involve two individuals who are doing all they can to be responsible to one another, to respect each other, willing to make compromise, accept their differences, and exercise self-control. We all must think about this.

Gaslighting is a terrible act that shouldn't be used. It's a mean, dehumanizing technique that has to be exposed for what it is so that people won't fall victim. Mental manipulation is evil, simple. Don't put up with it. It's never okay to be gaslighted by anybody—whoever it is.

CHAPTER THREE

NEGATIVE IMPACT OF NARCISSISTIC ABUSE ON FUTURE RELATIONSHIPS

I've earlier discussed several effects of narcissistic abuse on children in general. Now I want to narrow it down to its impact on future relationships. The good thing is that children of narcissistic parents won't live with their parents forever. The bad thing, unfortunately, is that the negative impacts of narcissistic abuse can be for a lifetime—if care isn't taken.

It was just yesterday we called today tomorrow - how time flies! The seed of yesterday has grown into a mighty tree. Time and tide wait for no man. No, I'm not in a proverbial mood, I'm just trying to pass the message on that everything is moving fast.

The girl who's raised by a narcissistic mom yesterday is now a beautiful woman, with children of her own. Does this frighten you or excite you? If it frightens you, I understand. And if it excites you, I also understand. It depends on where you are. It may frighten you because you feel you don't have enough time to heal, and it may excite you because it gives you hope that you'll soon separate from your mom.

Whichever side you are on, you should act fast by understanding the gimmicks of narcissists and how to hack them. Seek the help of a professional if you've been abused by a narcissistic mom, or by anyone at all.

I have to just break it to you—if you've been raised by a narcissistic mom, apart from the unpleasant consequences that you will have to go through, some of her narcissistic traits are very likely to rub off on you. This may be hard to stomach, especially if you're seeing the face of your mom yelling at you as you're reading this.

I don't want you to wave this off as a non-issue. It's a serious issue that needs sincere self-appraisal. I admit it may not be a comfortable thing to do, but the benefits are formidable and are proactive measures to help your relationships and mental wellbeing in the long run.

Children who are raised by narcissistic moms can be:

Arrogant and Cocky

Those who are raised by narcissistic moms tend to believe they are better and smarter than other people. They always carry this air of importance everywhere they go. They may not realize it unless their attention is called to it. If you find people often saying you're cocky or too full of yourself, and you've been raised by a narcissist, I'm afraid you're already exhibiting a trait of a narcissist.

If you find out that you're in the habit of giving people the cold shoulder or silent treatment, then you're already behaving like your mom. Self-confidence is good, but if people find your confidence annoying on a consistent basis, it may well be that your overconfidence is just a smokescreen of your arrogance.

One way to help yourself is by being conscious of your attitude. You may have to bring yourself to be sensitive to the needs of others. You can also ask your partner, friends, or those close to you to tell you what they don't like about you. Treasure their answers and act on them.

Indecisive and Gutless

It may be hard to have confidence in making decisions when you've lived with someone who always found fault with your decisions. How can you have trust in a person who's bent on making your life as miserable as hell? I truly get this. We shouldn't underestimate the ordeal those raised by narcissists are going through.

For victims of narcissism, the problem isn't in making decisions - they do make fantastic decisions—but it's in trusting their decisions. Often, they may find themselves in need of others' validations. This is what their experience with their narcissistic moms has done to them.

Because they've endured verbal abuse while growing up, victims of narcissism may lack the courage needed to quit an abusive relationship. They may convince themselves that it's not as bad as their relationship with their moms. It's a kind of Stockholm syndrome in which the hostage sympathizes with her captor.

A narcissistic mom has already set the bar of relationships so low for her child, that the child will see any of her future relationships in a better light, even if it's not beneficial to her. This is perhaps the chief reason why most victims of narcissistic abuse have problems in at least one of their romantic relationships.

Domineering and Bossy

When you lived with a domineering mom forever, it's so easy to be domineering yourself. The funny thing is that you may be too focused on your mom's domineering attitude that you won't see its ugly head rearing up in your own attitude.

Domineering people do so because they want to be in control. They want to tell people what to do and how to behave. They tell people what to eat, what to wear, where to go, when to go, what to say, and when to act. Nobody likes to be bossed about. This annoying attitude will no doubt affect the relationships of those who are into overbearing control of others.

If you think you're domineering, you'll have to be deliberate in allowing others to give their input. Be interested in what others have to say and be willing to execute their plans. Don't insist on getting your way all the time. This will be hard for you at first, but the law of adaption will soon take place. You'll be fine after a couple of trials. Remember, the trick is to be intentional about it.

Unrealistic and Demanding

To survive and be sane, victims of narcissistic abuse often withdraw into a world of fantasies. This enables them to switch from their pathetic role of a scapegoat to the enviable role of a golden lamb. Constantly finding safety in an unreal mental world can make them have unrealistic expectations.

And if their role is that of a golden child— narcissistic moms can make a child scapegoat or golden child (I'll explain this later)—the overpampering and adoration can make golden children see an unreal version of themselves. This distortion of reality can make them have unrealistic expectations.

Unrealistic expectations lead to unbelievable demands. Expectations are unrealistic because they are either mere wishes or unfeasible. Having unrealistic expectations is signing up for disappointment, because these expectations can't be met, at least to satisfaction. Having your unrealistic expectations unmet can make you act coldly to those you're in a relationship with.

Many victims of narcissism have an unrealistic expectation of a perfect marriage. They dream of a perfect person to spend the rest of their lives with. The problem with this expectation is that they will be disappointed because no one is perfect. This may be the reason why they keep on changing partners, hoping to find their perfect match.

Unfortunately, Cinderella and Tarzan aren't real, so don't pattern your dream partner on them, if you don't want to be disappointed. We all have one unrealistic expectation or the other, but some have them in excess. For instance, it's an unrealistic expectation when you expect everyone to like you or obey you. Unrealistic expectation: I can't make mistakes. Reality: You'll make mistakes because everyone does.

You can free yourself from the shackles of unrealistic expectations by being attentive to your demands and wants. This will require that you have to live in the real world more than you live in your imaginary world. You've got to accept life along with its striking realities.

Isolated and Empty

We feel empty when something vital is missing in our lives. We may feel empty when we don't have a sense of purpose when we are living our lives for others when our expectations aren't met when we've burned out, when we're addicted to alcohol and drugs, or when we're depressed.

It's not uncommon for victims of narcissistic abuse to feel empty every now and then. They often find themselves isolated, even among a crowd. The isolation feeling comes from the inability to relate with others socially. Those who are raised by narcissistic moms may not have the mental support needed to hone their communication skills and grow their confidence.

This dearth of vital life skills makes them shrink away from conversations, especially a one-on-one conversation. They fear public speaking and are always avoiding physical group chats. Even in social media group chats, you'll barely see their comments. Constantly feeling isolated will affect your mental health and your relationship with others.

To overcome these unkind feelings, you'll have to come out of your shell gently and boldly. You have to face your fears. There's nothing wrong with being lonely if you're cool with it. But if keeping to yourself makes you critical of yourself, then it's not good for you. You need to challenge yourself by taking bold steps to break free from your shell.

Narcissistic or even Sadistic

I've decided to save this for the last for obvious reasons. Several studies and anecdotal evidence have shown that victims of abuse can either come out hating the act of abuse or become abusers themselves. Constant exposure to abuse can cause the victim to endure the pain and in some rare cases, make her become an abuser.

Pain and vengeance can motivate a victim of abuse to become an abuser. For example, victims of narcissistic moms can end up enjoying sadistic narcissism. This can be actual enjoyment or vicarious enjoyment. The victims found the abuse repulsive at the outset. They were forced to develop thick skin to survive the trauma. Somewhere along the line, they became stoic, losing sensitivity and feelings for themselves. And when that happens, having feelings for others becomes an impossibility.

This is the most negative impact narcissism can have on a person. Treatment for this kind of person has to be for sadistic personality disorder and NPD. These people will have violent relationships. They will find pleasure in inflicting emotional and physical pain on people. It's a very serious case.

Finding a Partner

I have shown in many words, the negative effects and influences narcissistic moms have on their children. I have equally devoted several paragraphs to the devastating impacts these wrong influences have on relationships, be it with family members, friends, colleagues or acquaintances.

As a person raised by a narcissistic mom, you have to be extra careful about your romantic relationships. You've gone through so much, and you deserve better—you deserve not to go through another ordeal in your marriage. You deserve a good life and you deserve to enjoy the rest of your life.

However, there are certain steps you have to take to ensure this happens. You'll have to be in charge of your present. Your past has happened, so let it go. Some things are beyond your control in this life, and your past is one of them. We didn't get to choose our parents or nationality; we just found ourselves here. Even if we got to choose our parents, chances are we may have ended up choosing a home of a narcissist or another unpleasant home.

It's a very good thing that the present is in our hands. We can choose to live it or snooze through it. You can't do anything about your narcissistic mom, but you can do something about yourself. You can choose to keep allowing her to hurt you in person and thought, or you can choose to heal. You can choose to ignore your fears and feelings and let them control you or choose to listen to them and use them effectively.

Whichever you choose to do will surely affect your relationships, positively or negatively. The following are the steps you need to take when finding a partner:

Be Ready for a Relationship

This may sound obvious, but many people enter relationships before they are ready for them. By ready, I mean, you should be mentally and physically ready. Don't be intimidated or manipulated into a relationship. You know yourself best, so listen to your inner voice.

Sincerely evaluate yourself.

Ask yourself vocal questions: "Why do I want to enter this relationship?" "Am I truly ready?" "Does this person love me?" "Do I love this person?" "Is this person someone I can settle down with?" "Am I too reliant on this person?" "Am I caving in to pressure?" "Does he respect my privacy?"

Self-questioning is a proven method to determine one's true feelings about matters of the heart. It's alone time with your heart. But you've got to be honest in your answers. It's okay if some answers don't come on time. It may take hours, days, months, or even years to get answers, but please take your time. It's better to delay and make good decisions than make hasty decisions and suffer in the long run.

Your confidence and self-esteem increase when you evaluate yourself. You'll feel in control, and you'll be refreshed. Self-contemplation will also open your eyes to see the toxicity in your own life. It's so much easier to see the flaws in other people rather than in ourselves. But the truth is, as I guess you know, no one is perfect.

Self-assessment will help you see flaws you might have learned or developed during your time with your narcissistic mom. It will also help you make urgent corrections. This will require you to be more attentive to your character, words, and body language.

The ultimate aim of self-evaluation is to be ready emotionally, mentally, physically, and in every way. This is the number one thing you should do when you want to settle down with your significant other (S.O.).

Be Comfortable in Your Own Skin

I know you can't wait to settle down with your lovely partner. I'm quite happy for you! But I hope you're not settling down with your S.O. to flee from yourself. My genuine concern for you is because unrealistic expectations that a partner can complete us has led to many broken relationships and disappointments.

Relationships aren't a one-person thing. They involve two people who are equally committed to making it work. In other words, while your partner can compliment you, he can't complete you. Relationships are like a board game that requires two people, not a solo game that can be played by one person.

Don't enter a relationship thinking your partner will complete you or meet your emotional needs.

That will be one of the greatest mistakes of your life. Nobody can make you whole except your dear self. Nobody can fill your emotionally needs except you. The best your partner can do is to give you space and the support you need to meet your emotional needs. This is how he can compliment you.

You have to work on your self-perception before you start a relationship. Build your self-confidence and self-esteem before you enter a relationship. Don't depend on your partner to build it for you. In addition to that, your partner can even use your poor self-perception against you later. You can't be so sure. This is why you need to build your image yourself.

I'm not saying your partner can't support or encourage you. Why not? Please, go ahead and receive all the help and support you need, but know that the building is yours to do. The tip I'll give you is that you need to be comfortable in your own skin so that others' validations will only be a compliment, not a desperate need.

Don't lose yourself in your relationship because that's what your partner fell in love with. Don't prioritize your partner's needs at the expense of your own needs. You shouldn't relinquish your life goals and passions—I believe you have them—to please your partner. Never, ever do that! I repeat, never do that! Let your partner know about your goals and passions from the beginning.

If your partner can't support your goals, maybe it's time to say goodbye, as this could be a sign of incompatibility. Your partner should be comfortable with your passions and goals, and you should also be comfortable with his passions and goals. If this isn't the case, like I said earlier, it's time to say goodbye. If you don't say goodbye now, you'll likely say a difficult goodbye in the future.

Your passion is what gives you a sense of purpose, and dropping them to please someone will make you miserable later. So have that in mind when you're ready to say, "Yes, I do."

Express Yourself

If you feel you find it difficult to express yourself to your partner, then you shouldn't start a relationship with him just yet. Your difficulty in expression may not be his fault, it may be because of childhood experience, but it's still a good idea to pause and examine the cause.

The large doses of silent treatments and cold shoulders you were faithfully served during childhood no doubt have impaired your ability to express yourself confidently. But you'll have to understand that it's time you left your mother's shadow. Your partner isn't your mom, so be free with him.

Being in a relationship with someone you can't express your feelings, concerns, fears or displeasure is like being in prison.

That's the way I see it. Poor communication will lead to frustration for you and your partner. It will leave room for arguments, disappointments, bitterness, regrets, and even separation. Effective communication is the soul of every relationship.

I can't stress this point enough. Communication is the way individuals get to know themselves better. But when this is missing, that relationship will be stormy. Instead of it to heal you, it will end up making you worse. So, please, I beg you, make every effort to communicate clearly.

Be Yourself

Don't pretend to be who you're not because you'll eventually get tired of being someone else. An African adage says, "Personality is like flame, it'll certainly find its way out." This is very true! Anyway, what's the point of pretending or trying to be who you're not? If your partner doesn't like your true self, don't manipulate him into like it. Let him go if he wants to.

It's alright if he likes hanging out with friends and you don't like it. Let him know you don't like it and tell him why you don't like it. You don't have to binge-watch movies if movies aren't your thing. Let him know. Your partner might like drinking, and you don't like it, let him know.

I'm not in any way encouraging inflexibility or arrogance. And I'm not against change. All I'm saying is this: don't change for him when it's not beneficial for you. Of course, if the change is beneficial for you, please adapt to it. Binge-watching isn't beneficial to you; drugs or drinks aren't beneficial to you. You get my point?

Don't engage in sexual practices that you aren't comfortable with, all in the name of changing for your partner. It's okay if you don't like his style of music, so don't force yourself to listen. Partners who demand changes like this are self-centered and arrogant. You may have to think again about your relationship with them.

This also applies to you. Allow your partner to be himself. Don't force him to change to his preferences, unless they are something he'll benefit from. Your partner may not be a game freak, so don't force him. Let him be himself. There's beauty in diversity. You don't want to marry yourself, or do you? So let your partner have his differences.

Narcissistic Traits and Tendencies in your Own Parenting

As rational beings, we learn directly and indirectly. You may not realize it, but each of your sense is always picking up information and sending them to the brain for processing. This is happening all the time! Your ears send what they hear to the brain, even when you're not actively listening. You may find a particular unfamiliar song replaying in your mind at night when you're about to rest, only for you to remember you heard the song on your way to work that morning.

Your eyes also send information they receive to the brain for processing. Many things are recorded when you look, but you only see, that is, take notice of what your brain has processed. This is why a particular object might catch your attention for the first time on your way to work, even though you've been using that route for years. What has just happened is that the brain has processed that particular object.

It's the same for all our senses. The point I'm driving at is that we can learn a habit without realizing it until it's fully manifested. Several studies confirm this point. Children generally and inevitably pick one or two attitudes of their parents simply by unconscious emulation. You can pick a habit or behavior by simply seeing your mom do it over and over again.

The character of those with whom we spend a considerable part of our lives tends to rub off on us. This is an indisputable fact. This fact is both a blessing and a curse. It's a blessing if we pick the good habits, and it's a curse if we pick the bad habits. The way forward to avoiding bad characters and habits rubbing off on us is to stand guard and be at alert.

It's always a hard pill to swallow for victims of narcissistic abuse to see traits of their narcissistic moms in them. They see themselves acting in cocky and insensitive manners like their moms. They see themselves always wanting to dominate their partners and children. They want their say to be final, just like their moms.

This realization often makes them more miserable than they already are. They can hate themselves and feel extremely very guilty that they are doing to their partner or children what their moms did to them. But at the same time, they may want to rationalize and justify their narcissistic behaviors. This isn't good.

Watch out for the things your mom did. This will require constant frank self-evaluation sessions and some actions.

Talk to a Therapist

If you feel you're exhibiting some narcissistic behaviors that you detest in your mom, you need to talk to a therapist. This is very urgent. Don't delay. The danger is that the more you rationalize your bad attitudes, the more time it will take to drop them. So seek the help of a professional as soon as possible. Please.

It can be really depressing and heart-shattering for a victim of narcissistic abuse to see herself acting just like her mom. Knowing that you're acting like your mom, of all people on this globe, can cause you to be anxious. You have to try therapy with a professional. Don't think you can handle this on your own.

It will be very difficult for you to do on your own because you're swinging from being critical of yourself to rationalizing your narcissistic attitudes. A good therapist will walk you through your conscious and unconscious knowledge about your experiences.

As you talk together, both of you will come to see the reason for the negative influence. It may be that you're unconsciously craving your mother to love and respect you for once, and this is the embryonic cord connecting you to the matrix of your mother's negativities. I hate to break it to you, but there's a chance your narcissistic mom may never change. So you just have to let go and enjoy the love of those who cherish you.

Put your Mom in her Place

This subheading may sound somehow odd to you, but it's perhaps the most important tip you should remember when finding a partner. Don't give your mom's ugly campaigns enough airtime in your mind. Don't always think about her abuse. The ironic thing I've come to observe is that children of narcissistic moms give their mom more attention than they like to admit or realize.

It doesn't matter that you're always thinking about a person negatively or positively; the fact remains that the person is always in your thoughts. It's like the media always reporting negative things about politicians. The reality is that the more reports, negative or positive, on a person, the more spotlight and exposure you give him.

So the more negatively you think about your mom, the more the platform you give her in your life. The more the power and control you give her. It's not just enough to give your narcissistic mom a physical space; you also have to give her a mental space. And if you are seeking my opinion, the mental space is the more important of the two. I'll explain more on this later.

Make efforts to detach from your unpleasant experiences with your mom. These thoughts are negative energy that are capable of turning you into version 2.0 of your mom if you allow it. You're not your mom, and you're not her creation. Your mom has lived her life, and now is the time for you to live yours.

Don't Overdo It

It's usual for victims of narcissistic abuse to want to be oversensitive and hyper-alert to situations around them. Being too conscious of your mother's parenting style can make you go overboard in your own parenting. You may want to love your child excessively because you don't want him to lack the motherly love you lacked.

It's also not unusual to want to overprotect your child. The problem with overprotection is that it can easily lead to overpampering and domineering. Before you realize it, you're dictating everything your partner or child should do and not do, because you don't want them to get hurt like you.

This is a good intention, but the strategy is harmful. You'll only end up choking your loved ones with excess of everything. Your ultra-care can easily become intrusive and toxic to your child. So be moderate in how you dish out your care and love. One way to do this is to respect your child's privacy and know what he wants. Don't assume you know his needs.

Don't be Afraid to Learn from the Past

You can't deny your past, though you can choose to ignore it. Whether you acknowledge your childhood or refute it, when you become a parent, you'll unconsciously relate with your child based on your own childhood experiences. Since this is case, why not intentionally reference your past so that you can avoid the mines and pitfalls your parents stepped on?

You don't have to live in the past, letting it affect you negatively. Regardless of what happened, you can be a good parent to your child. You can be a role model to other victims. You can come out of this strongly. But you must be bold enough to face your past and learn from it. Facing your past gives you the confidence to face the future. This is how it works.

Stop Blaming your Parents

It's so easy to blame others for our woes, but it's very difficult to take responsibility when we point accusing fingers at our malefactors. If you want to be in charge of your life, be a good parent to your child, and a good partner to your S.O., you've got to stop blaming your parents.

Of course, you should recognize the negative influence your parents had on you, but don't cling to the hurt or keep bashing them. Your sanity depends on this. Holding on the hurts of the past can negatively affect how you relate to your child. You may find yourself hurting your child in the process. Let it go!

Chapter Summary

Narcissistic abuse affects its victims in terrible ways. It affects their whole outlook on life. It rears its ugly head in relationships and parenting. Victims of this kind of abuse find it difficult to cope with romantic relationships, with their children, and with people in general.

What's more terrifying is the prospect of them acting like their narcissistic parents. This is a scary thing for them. The last person they ever wanted to emulate is their mother, but they can't help it. The help of a therapist is crucial to treatment.

CHAPTER FOUR

THE NARCISSIST FAMILY SETTING

I'm devoting this chapter to let you have an idea of what a home controlled by a narcissist looks like. It's a very interesting family setting. If one of your parents is a narcissist, I guess you know the setting already. Narcissists are control freaks, so it's not unusual that they assign different roles to their family members.

These roles are hostile to one another. A narcissist thrives where there's division. She enjoys watching competition among family members, as long as no one is competing against her. Before I proceed, I'm conspicuously assigning the narcissist role to the mom.

The narcissist can be a parent, a sibling, a grandparent, or a close relative. I've said a lot about the narcissist, so I won't say much about her here. The other roles in a typical narcissistic family are:

The Enabler

This is the non-narcissistic parent, in our scenario - the dad. The enabler, also called codependent, is called so, not because he instigates his wife's narcissism, but because he does nothing to stop her. His ideal fatherly role is to assuage the impacts of his wife's toxicity on their children. But for some reason—or rather, weaknesses—best known to him, he helplessly watches as the hegemon wreaks her havoc.

Though he's not the culprit, he's an accomplice. His complicity is that he encourages the narcissistic abusive behavior of his wife by his silence and his turning of the blind eye. In fact, the abused children may hate the enabler as much as they hate the narcissist—or even more than they hate the narcissist.

The enabler can also be a grandparent, an uncle or close family member who resides in the house or spend time with the family. The enabler embraces his role for various reasons, such as being victimized and treated harshly by the command-in-chief (the narcissist) or being manipulated into believing the agenda and narrative of the narcissist or just for selfish reasons.

In some cases, the enabler goes as far as defending the narcissistic actions of the narcissist. His reasons for doing this may be that he's simply tired of being frustrated by the narcissist, he's expecting something from the narcissist, or he wants to earn the trust of the narcissist.

Whatever his reasons are, he's shooting himself in the foot. His cowardice will later catch up with him. He'll later realize, often too late, that narcissists can't be trusted or pleased and that he should've stood up to his abusive wife. The enabler is as much a victim as the golden child and the scapegoat.

If you realize you've been enabling your narcissistic partner all along, it's time you stopped. It's something you'll later regret. But you've got to brace yourself up for the biggest confrontation of your life. The narcissist will pull the hordes of hell to fight you. She'll frustrate you and withhold certain privileges you've enjoyed during your role as a codependent in a bid to bring you to your knees.

But don't cave in. Think about the bigger picture. Think about the negative impacts her narcissism is having on your children and loved ones, and most importantly, think about your own future. Do you want to be lonely at the end of your life or do you want to be surrounded by your lovely kids? Like it or not, everyone wants to be loved and checked after in old age.

The Golden Child

We now come to mom's favorite. The perks for this position are great, but the downside to this role is its insecurity. The golden child remains golden like the sun for as long as he/she kowtows to the narcissist. The golden child is the ideal child of the narcissist. In the opinion of the narcissist, the golden child can do no wrong. His/her intelligence and actions are exaggerated. He/she's praised for nothing.

The narcissistic mom sees herself in the golden child. She makes her be what she wants to be, acts in ways she wants to act, and carry out duties that serve her agenda. In return, the golden child gets the attention and the gifts. The golden child does few chores or no chores at all.

These are exaggerated affections, ostentatiously done to intimidate and tease belligerent family members. They are carefully stage-managed so that others, especially the scapegoat child, may see the privileges the golden child enjoys. This is a terrible parenting style, by the way.

The golden child is often pitted against other siblings; this hostility further serves the selfish cause of the narcissist. The golden child gives the narcissist a false impression that she's a good mom. In her thinking, the golden child is her only child. She doesn't really acknowledge the scapegoat child as a child.

To avoid conflict in the house, the enabler also has to pamper the golden child. Even if he doesn't like the golden child, he just has to pretend he does. The golden child is lucky. Right? Not really. Don't envy the golden child. The golden child may think she's the favorite child, but this isn't true.

The narcissist is using her more as an accessory and a weapon rather than as a child. She's only a tool in her mother's hand. If she really wants to see whether the love and care she's been getting are genuine or not, she should refuse to do the bidding of her narcissistic mom and see what happens.

Like I said earlier, the golden child is only golden for as long as she complies with her mother's directives. The narcissistic mom won't think twice before she demotes the golden child. She'll strip her of her privileges and give them to another who's worthy—or willing to submit to her lordship. This may hurt the feelings of the exgolden child, but a narcissist doesn't care about others' feelings.

If you're the golden child of your family, you should quit that role. Continuing in that role will keep making your narcissistic mom stronger, and the stronger she becomes, the more toxic she becomes. Don't underestimate the range of her narcissistic missiles. I understand that it's going to be a tough decision to make, but you just have to do it for the sake of your siblings and loved ones and yourself.

You can start by politely declining to do your mom's dirty job. Have a mind of your own. This will definitely take her aback and she may be rattled, but be strong and keep your stand. Be prepared for repercussions and a change of fortunes. It will be a hard time, but you'll come out stronger.

The Scapegoat

And here comes our protagonist, the only person with guts in the family. The scapegoat is the child who doesn't dance to the tunes of her narcissistic moms. She's always the center of wrath and fury. Nothing she does is ever right. She's punished for nothing. In her mother's opinion, she doesn't know how to do anything.

She's punished and accused of everything.

She's punished for the narcissist's disappointments, the enabler's errors, and the golden child's failures.

She does the chores and run the errands.

She's always receiving the cold treatment. If you call her an outcast, you wouldn't be wrong. This is the price she has to pay for having a mind of her own.

Think of the child in the scapegoat role as the exact opposite of the golden child. While the golden child is the target of the narcissist's love and gifts, the scapegoat child is the target of her raw rage and fury. She's also the guinea pig of the family. She's the first to try out unpleasant things and the last to try pleasant things.

The reason the narcissist doesn't have a good relationship with the scapegoat child is because the child is a constant threat. The scapegoat child is vocal in her criticism and honest opinions; narcissists don't like that. The scapegoat child is a mini activist in the house; she fights for the rights of weak family members.

All this threatens narcissists. They will do all they can to pile pressure on their critics to silence them.

This is why the narcissistic mom makes a scapegoat out of the outspoken child. She does this to break her willpower. She may even try to bribe the child by suddenly being nice to her. If she really needs the outspoken child on her side, she may even offer to make her a golden child.

It doesn't take a narcissist a second to discard or employ. The page that has the word "loyalty" is missing in her dictionary. Remember, she'll do all she can to get you to worship her, but don't be tempted.

If you're the scapegoat child in your family, don't give up. Keep fighting for what you believe is right. Don't be intimidated or bullied into doing what will advance the agenda of the narcissist. Educate yourself so that you can defend yourself against gaslighting.

The Flying Monkey

The flying monkey (coined from the movie "The Wizard of Oz") is the mercenary the narcissist uses to execute her dirty jobs, knowingly or unknowingly. This person is usually manipulated by the narcissist to advance her cause. The flying monkey spies on those who are in the black book of the narcissist.

His job is also to portray the narcissist in good light to others and to badmouth her detractors. The flying monkey can be a sibling, a relative, friend, or colleagues. But, preferably, he has to have a relationship with the target of the narcissist. The narcissist will directly or indirectly be using him against her victim. But flying monkeys are often exploited and used against victims of the narcissist, with whom they have a working relationship with.

Breaking the Hegemony of a Narcissist

To defeat the narcissist in your family, all of you must come together to counter her. Unity is key in diluting the toxic influence of a narcissist. Don't think that you're immune to the negative influence of a narcissist. Whether you're an enabler, a golden child, or a child in a scapegoat role, each role has its unique negative influences.

The enabler or codependent may find himself exhibiting some narcissistic behaviors of his partner. He may find himself in the middle someday, and he'll receive all the blame. The children will blame him for his inaction and complicity. Even his narcissistic wife will blame him for... anything that comes to her mind at that time.

Apart from the risk of becoming a narcissist, the golden child is also in danger of becoming hypersensitive and risk losing herself, her self-image and self-confidence. The golden child may also end up becoming just like her narcissistic mom because she allowed herself to be her projection.

The scapegoat child, though having a mind of her own, may end up becoming insensitive and embittered. She may find herself overreacting to situations. The risks of character flaws developed by either direct or indirect emulation, or by offensive or defensive response are high with family members of a narcissist. This is why everyone has to unite together to debilitate the negative energy of a narcissist.

Chapter Summary

Narcissists gain and subsist on dominance through division. Their ideology seeks to divide and rule. They find it difficult to orchestrate their program where there's harmony. A united front chokes them. If you have family members who are willing to cooperate with you, good for you. It's in your interest to join hands together and defend your souls.

If you don't have family members who see things as you do or don't want to cooperate, you should watch out for yourself.

CHAPTER FIVE

PUBLIC AND PRIVATE IMAGES OF NARCISSISTS

Narcissists are good actors.

This is one of their manipulative skills. They need histrionic skills to gaslight their victims and assert their dominance. The better you understand their good acting skills, the better you'll be able to deal with them.

Narcissists can be charming when they want to. I mean, they are great charmers! They have the uncanny ability to sweep you off your feet on a first encounter. You'll love them! They are astute in reading their scripts and in interpreting their roles perfectly well. That's why they are good actors!

And what're their scripts? You and me. Their scripts are people they meet and situations they find themselves. They will enchant you if they need something from you. They may like something or dislike it, depending on the script. For example, a narcissist may actually dislike your taste in music but can tell you she loves you to get to you.

A narcissist can pretend to like your favorite celebrity if that will help her cause. I have to warn you; narcissists are good actors—better than Angelina Jolie and Dwayne Johnson combined. Okay, that may be an exaggeration. But you get my point? Good, that's all that matters.

You really have to understand this aspect of narcissists, because this is one aspect people don't really know about them. And this is why people, even some relatives and friends, don't know the ordeal a child is going through at home. The reason is that the narcissist is playing the role of the best mom outside and the villain at home.

So I'll be devoting this chapter to revealing their various images and roles. I could write a whole book on this alone. To help you have a concrete understanding of the acting skills of narcissists, I'll be using tangible imageries to explain.

The Human Chameleon

Narcissists change attributes more than chameleons. That comparison may be hyperbolic, but it's not that off if you've met a narcissist. Chameleons change color for various reasons: to adapt to their environments: to adjust their body temperature to that of their environment, to trap unsuspecting prey and to protect themselves from predators.

Does this sound familiar? Narcissist acts to:

Adapt to their Environments

Like chameleons, narcissists need to adapt to their environments before they begin their operations properly. This is the first thing they do. Don't let their self-absorption and insensitivity fool you into thinking they don't know what's going on around them. They do!

They do more than you realize, and this is one of their advantages. It takes dark wisdom to foster division between people. It takes some ingenuity to gaslight and exploits others for selfish purposes. So wake up from your slumber! Narcissists are much more alert to their environment.

They are great readers of situations and good calculators. They may appear slow like chameleons, but their shrewdness makes up for their seeming tardiness. To adapt to their environment, narcissists do a lot of script reading.

Adjust their Body Temperature to that of their Environment

While chameleons adjust their body temperature to match that of their environment, narcissists adjust their mood and character to match that of those around them who they stand to benefit from. Narcissists will never adjust their mood for those they can bully.

This ability endears narcissists to outsiders. A woman can be a narcissist in her home, and no one in her church may know anything about it. They are that good! Your narcissistic mom may put up her best behavior in public, to the admiration of everyone—including you. You may find yourself wondering if this is actually your mom. She has mastered the art of playing the part.

Trap Unsuspecting Prey

Have you seen the chameleon's tongue before? It's a long thingy that's super-fast. The chameleon uses it to draw in unsuspecting prey into the vaults of its stomach. Narcissists are like this too. They may not be fast as chameleons, but like their reptile counterparts, their attack is sudden and fast.

They first start by disguising themselves as good people. They will make every effort to make their victims feel comfortable before they strike. It's like the proverbial folklore in which the animal kingdom decided to kill the proud elephant. The only way to do this was to make the elephant the king.

Amidst pomp and pageantry, they led the elephant to the throne that was placed on a very deep hole. Thud! The big guy crashed into the hole trumpeting as he went down. That was the end of that elephant. Moral of the story: The narcissist doesn't mind making you a king if that's how he'll get rid of you.

Protect themselves from Predators

Though narcissists live in an imaginary world, they understand the dangers of real life. This is to be expected since the trauma of real life was what encouraged their narcissism in the first place. If pretending to be who they are not will protect their dominance and selfish interests, they will do it.

They can even obey or submit themselves for the time being to protect themselves. But be assured that they will strike at the opportune moment, and they will strike hard.

Having multiple images is essential for the survival of narcissists; it's their way of being in control.

They require a public image and a private image to be on top of their game. Their public image is a nice, easygoing, and lovely one. This isn't their true nature. It's a false projection of their true self. The private image, on the other hand, is who they truly are. Your true character is the quality you exhibit when you're alone. It's pure and unpretentious.

Typical Images of Narcissists

Narcissists can be compared to many things. Narcissists are:

Like the Earth

Narcissists are like the earth. How? Glad you asked. The earth is dark on one side and bright on the other side. This explains night and day. When the United States is sunny, the United Kingdom will be moony. As the earth spins around its own axis, one side faces the sun, and the other side backs the sun. The side that faces the sun is the day and the other side is the night.

Narcissists spin around their own axis too! They show a good side to some and bad side to others, depending on their mood, relationship, and selfish interest.

Their public image is sunny, lovely and beautiful to behold. You'd love it. But their private image is often dark and freezing cold. This is their true nature.

Their dark side is insensitive, emotionless, abusive, divisive, domineering, cocky, and every other trait

I've addressed earlier about NDP. This is the hidden side, but it's the side that's venomous.

Demons at Home

On their good day, narcissists can be very cruel, but on a bad day, they can be monstrous. This image is, of course, shown to those close to them. It's their private image. They are venomous monsters that victimize their victims. They are unstoppable in their quest to assert their dominance.

They are merciless and vicious.

They will do almost anything to achieve their objectives.

They will gaslight, victimize, traumatize, and even pauperize to have their way.

Show me a more formidable monster!

Angels Outside

Narcissists are angels on the outside. They are likable and social. They are good actors, remember? Outsiders see them as those who wouldn't even hurt a fly. They are congenial and fun to be with. This unreal side of them is part of their divisive strategy. They need to put on a show so that outsiders won't suspect a thing.

Chapter Summary

Image is everything to narcissists. They need this talent for survival and dominance. Please, never underestimate the acting skills of narcissists. If your mom is a narcissist, or you know a narcissist, you've already seen it in action.

Narcissists must have two images: a public image and a private image. The images you see are the ones they want you to see. They are like chameleons, so they can neatly hide their flaws. They can pretend to be who they aren't perfectly because their whole life is imaginary. You must be very careful when you're dealing with them.

CHAPTER SIX

DIFFERENCE BETWEEN NARCISSISTIC TRAITS AND NPD

So far in this book, you'd have observed that I have sometimes used the term "narcissist" and "narcissism" as a short way to refer to those with NDP. I just thought I should point that out. I must explain what healthy narcissistic traits are and are not.

Frankly speaking, everyone exhibits some narcissistic traits. We may get carried away sometimes and go into self-absorption. There are times during decision-making that we just focus on ourselves without considering the impacts of our decisions on others.

There are also times our ego set in, and we feel we are more important and indispensable than other people. These are examples of narcissistic traits. I could go on to give several traits of narcissism. So you can see that everyone has the tendency to be narcissistic.

Whenever you see yourself as profoundly more important than other people, you're exhibiting a narcissistic trait. Are these narcissistic traits necessarily evil? Not really if you don't go overboard with it. You're not going overboard if you don't exhibit them all the time and if your actions or words don't hurt others emotionally or physically.

Exhibiting some narcissistic traits doesn't mean you have NDP. As I explained in the *Introduction* of this book, a person with NDP has narcissism as a prevalent behavior. This means that people with NDP are chronically given to narcissistic traits. It's not a one-shot exhibition of narcissistic traits for them. Narcissism has become their nature, their way of life. They've come to rely on narcissism as a means of survival.

Modern appeal for narcissistic traits has challenged the traditional view on narcissism. Pop psychology, while agreeing that narcissism is destructive and abusive, argues that narcissism also has its good side. It argues, though cautiously, that healthy narcissism can boost self-esteem and increase productivity.

The question, then, is: how can narcissism be healthy and beneficial? Opinions vary, and understandably so, on the benefits of narcissism.

The major problem many scholars have with the concept of "healthy narcissism" is its paradoxical outlook—and advocates of healthy narcissism appear to agree that it sounds paradoxical.

The bone of contention is: How can anything good come out of narcissism (self-centeredness)? How can being egoistically concerned with oneself to the detriment of others be healthy? How can self-obsession, which denies the greater good of others, be healthy? You get the point now?

My personally opinion is that narcissism, by its core definition and characterizations, isn't healthy. Some may not agree with this, and I'm cool with it. I agree that some narcissistic traits, like overconfidence, egoism, arrogance, ruthlessness, can increase productivity and make one successful. In fact, several studies have found that many successful leaders exhibit some narcissistic traits.

I think the misconception about the benefits of narcissism comes from interchanging narcissistic traits with narcissism. What many simply call "narcissism" are traits of narcissism. They mean a narcissistic person is someone who's egoistic and arrogant. This is true, but it's not the bigger picture.

I understand the problem some have with labeling people as "narcissistic." Our society has come to label anyone who's arrogant, cocky, and often successful as a narcissist. This cheap serving of narcissism has muddled the true meaning of narcissism. As I said, it's better to set the difference between narcissistic traits and narcissism, which is the prevalent behavior of NPD.

A person can be cocky and arrogant and may be struggling with another personality disorder. So narcissistic traits aren't limited to narcissism alone. Based on this line of reasoning, I'll say again that narcissism is never healthy—never! Don't let anyone deceive you that narcissism is good.

Now I'm not saying it's wrong to feel more important than others; you should. Why not! But you shouldn't be obsessed with it. It shouldn't be hurting or belittling others. You can be resolute without being a brute. Enjoy the rhyme, but get the point. You can have your way without stepping on toes. Right? I thought so, too.

You can dominate and not be domineering, just as you can win a game without cheating. Learn to be a good listener and avoid trying to tell people what to do all the time. Narcissistic traits may be helpful at the beginning, but you will find they don't help forever.

You may count on narcissistic traits to help you get into a relationship you so desired, but they won't help you sustain it. Healthy personality traits are what will help and sustain your position of authority, relationship, and emotional intelligence. Please, don't count on narcissistic traits to do this for you. It will be like building a house out of straw. It will all come crashing down soon.

Like I said earlier, low sugar levels and high sugar level are both harmful to the body. Sugar level has to be moderate. It's the same with narcissistic traits. Do everything with moderation.

Types of Narcissists

That said, I want to address another important point. Having said a lot about narcissists and people living NPD, I should let you know more about the two types of narcissists there are. This will better help you to know how to deal with narcissists in your life. The two types are:

The "Good" Narcissist

This narcissist may not be aware she has NPD, but she's aware that she hurts others. She may be defensive when she's accused of being rigidly insensitive and extremely self-centered, but deep down in her, she wants to do good things, but she's helpless about her situation. This narcissist is really trying to be selfless and care about others, but she seems restrained by some forces.

These forces are webs of negative adaptations from her childhood. The abuse she went through during her formative years impelled her to protect herself by self-absorption that she just can't see from anyone's perspective other than hers. She knows she's hurting other people; at times, she's concerned and other times she's not. She finds herself juggling between guilt for her horrible behavior and justifying her selfish actions. She may react offensively when accosted for her behaviors.

This narcissist unintentionally causes harm to others. This is why I've decided to call her a "good narcissist." This label doesn't excuse her horrible attitudes, and I'm not in any way justifying her wicked actions. Not at all. Her actions, while often not done on purpose, are still as scarring and hurtful as those perpetrated by the bad narcissist. The only difference is that the good narcissist doesn't take pleasure in her narcissistic venom.

But she can't help herself. She finds it difficult and impossible to stop herself. Mind you, I'm not saying that the good narcissist doesn't do all the bad stuff that is typical of narcissists, she does them, but she doesn't feel good about it. But this not-feel-good feeling isn't strong enough to stop her from orchestrating her agenda.

A good narcissist will do things that will hurt your feelings without having the slightest inkling that their actions are hurting you. Her joke on you may be very offensive, but she doesn't know that. Narcissists generally don't have empathy. They are very poor in understanding the point of view of another person or know or recognize or appreciate the feelings of others.

In a relaxed and calm mood, the good narcissist may realize she's wrong, but her delicate self-esteem will not let her apologize. To apologize is admitting that she's wrong, and narcissists are never wrong. They may not be right, but they are never wrong. You understand that, right? She'd rather make warm gestures than admit she's wrong. But if the other person is proud enough to reject her privileged offer, her ego would be hurt, and the misunderstanding would begin all over again.

The good narcissist will still gaslight if she has to, manipulate when she has to, attack emotionally and physically if she wants to. She's still her callous, coldhearted self. My point is: in all this, she still wishes she could stop being bad. So in conclusion, the good narcissist is good because she knows she's bad. I believe this punch line clears away all confusion.

It's in the best interest of good narcissists to get themselves treated by the use of psychotherapy. I'm sure by now that you'll know if your mom is a good narcissist or a bad one. I hope this will guide you in your approach to healing and your relationship with your mom.

The Badass Narcissist

The badass narcissist is bad because she knows she's bad, and she enjoys being bad. She prides herself as a hurting machine. The bad narcissist hurts others on purpose. She takes pleasure in casting others down, letting them know their inferior place. She does this both in unintentional and intentional ways.

At least the good narcissist realizes her hurtful actions or words, but is too self-oriented to tender an apology. The bad narcissist doesn't recognize and doesn't even care to recognize her wrong. So thinking of how to repair the damage she's caused is completely anathema to her.

The bad narcissist is ready to do anything to have everything. She's a professional in stepping on toes. Her cruelty knows no bounds if sadism is also involved. She takes pleasure in hurting and devaluing people. She thrives on belittling others. She objectifies people and treats them as mere accessories.

The summation is this: The badass narcissist doesn't care about their actions and words, and least of all, about the feelings of others. The sadistic one even enjoys playing with people's feelings to manipulate and hurt them. The good narcissist, on the other hand, tries to be good but is inhibited by the core traits of narcissism. I believe you now know the type of narcissist your mom is, and I hope this knowledge soothes you and help you on your course to finding yourself.

Two Categories of Narcissists

Before I end this chapter, I must call your attention to the two categories of narcissism there are. Just as there are two types of narcissists, there are also two categories of narcissists. Every narcissist falls into either of the categories I'll address now. The dominant state of narcissism can either be grandiose or hypertensive.

In other words, in every narcissist, you'll either see the overbearing characteristics of grandiosity or vulnerability. These dominant traits determine the willpower and the volatile strength of a narcissist.

Now let's see what these two categories are:

Grandiose Narcissist

The grandiose narcissist is arrogant, defiant, and pompous. Children who were treated as superior during their childhood are more susceptible to grandiosity than those who were neglected. So golden children are more likely to be grandiose than children who were the scapegoats.

She doesn't see herself as the prey but as the predator. Seeing herself as the victim makes her weak and doesn't synchronize with her superior mentality. The grandiose narcissist has an unrealistic sense of superiority, and she sees herself as better than everyone else.

The sole drive the grandiose narcissist is her belief that she'll be great in life. She desires more than anything else to be famous and powerful, and she'll take on anyone or anything that stands in her way or threatens her greatness. She's ready to do anything to be great, and she'll do anything to get recognition.

This narcissist is very adventurous. She has high expectations about everything and goes out of her way to get them met. She's not afraid to make demands or express herself. Unlike the vulnerable narcissist, she doesn't mind being criticized. She could easily dismiss criticism as an expression of another person's envy. In fact, criticism seems to fuel her resolution.

All this makes it easy for the grandiose narcissist to leave any relationship they feel isn't patting their egoistic back. Besides, she considers all those in her life lucky and privileged, because she sees herself as indispensable. Her reasoning is that her partner, if she's in a romantic relationship, her colleagues and even her boss are all lucky to have her.

One keyword to remember about a grandiose narcissist, if you can't remember anything else, is "unconscionable." A grandiose narcissist is extremely bad, unfair, impudent, imprudent, and lack conscience.

Vulnerable Narcissist

The vulnerable narcissist is vulnerable, but she's no less dangerous than the grandiose narcissist. Have you heard of the adage "a green snake in the green grass" or for short "a snake in the grass?" Think of the vulnerable narcissist as one. The only reason she's described as vulnerable is because she's too sensitive. Does the word "cry baby" cross your mind? If it does, you aren't wrong.

You have to be very careful about what you say and what you don't say when you are around a vulnerable narcissist because she's watching your every move—your eye movement, mouth shape, toe-tapping, smile, laughter. I'm telling you, she's hypersensitive.

You'll have to think twice before praising her because she may think you're being sarcastic. And you have even to think thrice before you criticize her. While like a typical narcissist, a vulnerable narcissist doesn't care about others' emotions, but she cares so much about her own emotions.

This narcissist alternates can be so moody. One time she is like a lion, whose roar sends shivers waving through the jungle, and at other times she's the rat, who could barely intimidate ants. Her fragile self-esteem is based on the events of her life. Unlike the grandiose narcissist, she's not immune to negative feedback. She's not a fighter.

This narcissist needs continued validation of others to fuel her self-esteem. She'll want her partner or colleague to tell her good and positive things. She'll try all her best to avoid criticism because that's her worst fear. If someone challenges her ability or corrects her, she'll feel really bad.

Her reaction to criticism will be based on the mood of the time, which the challenger is, and the weight of the issue. She may quit her job; she may file for a divorce or storm out of the relationship or she may harm her child or do anything impulsive.

Because of her extremely poor self-esteem, the vulnerable narcissist has difficulty in trusting others. She'll see all-female friends of her partner as a threat. She'll always read beyond the lines. Her vulnerability will make her see what's not there. The grandiose narcissist is a good fault finder, both real faults and unreal faults. But she'll never accept that she's fallible. She won't take any criticism lightly.

For example, she may suspect her partner is having an affair with another person and accuse him of this, though her suspicion may be baseless and untrue; and this is even though she's having an affair or affairs herself. If her partner finds out about this and confronts her, she'll react defensively and make the whole thing all about her partner.

Those who were neglected by their parents during childhood or children who were the scapegoats in a narcissistic family are more susceptible to vulnerable narcissism.

Treatment for NPD

I have a feeling you really want to know the prognosis of NPD. Many sicknesses are curable, and some aren't. We can't really say that NPD is curable, and we also can't say that it's not curable. It is treatable. But whether the prognosis will be favorable or not has a lot to do with the cooperation of the narcissist.

The only known and feasible treatment of NPD is psychotherapy, which utilizes and encourages dialogue rather administering drugs. As of now, no drug treats NPD though drugs may be prescribed for other related problems such as depression and insomnia.

During the psychotherapy session, the psychologist will calmly ask questions and allow the person with NPD also to ask questions. The aim is to find the underlying cause of the NPD and how it can be managed. But as you have probably have asked, would the narcissist submit herself for therapy?

It would be very difficult for a narcissist to go for therapy because that would mean she recognizes that she needs help. This show of weakness is something even vulnerable narcissists won't want to do. This is why many think that NPD is incurable. It's always a great challenge for family members or friends of a narcissist to convince them of their need for treatment.

This requires time, patience, and wisdom. But have it in mind before you approach your narcissistic mom that she may never accept that she needs help—and understand that this move can cause more upset in your already tensioned relationship.

NPD is treatable—if the narcissist is willing to cooperate. It will, however, take extraordinary willpower for a narcissist to submit herself to therapy. Most times, a life-changing event must have happened for this to happen. But for those who commit themselves to therapy, they can gradually learn empathy.

They can pragmatically and lovingly be made to have realistic expectations and made to see how their actions and words have been hurting their relationships. However, recovery from NPD will be very slow. Family of the narcissist will also have to be patient and not raise their hopes too high, as full recovery isn't guaranteed.

Chapter Summary

Narcissism isn't the same as exhibiting narcissistic traits. It's important to understand the differences. Everyone exhibits narcissistic traits from time to time, but that doesn't mean everyone has NPD. In fact, only a handful of the population has NPD.

The arguments for and against what healthy narcissism is, or if narcissism is healthy at all, will be put to rest if all parties see the need for moderation. Some prefer to call NPD "pathological narcissism" rather than just calling it narcissism. Whichever term we would like to call it, we should all know that narcissism is a prevalent trait in NPD.

Also, understanding the types of narcissists there are can, perhaps, make you heal better. But it may also help you to understand that not all narcissists hurt on purpose.

While the expressions are different, both the grandiose narcissist and the vulnerable are both self-serving and dangerous. The grandiose narcissist attracts people because of her high confidence and determination, and the vulnerable narcissist attracts people because of her calm and reserved personality.

It's impossible to say which category if more dangerous, as both are capable of an assailing narcissistic rage that is capable of wreaking tangible and intangible havoc. It's so easy to categorize the good narcissist as a vulnerable narcissist and the bad narcissist as the grandiose narcissist, but this isn't always true.

While the good narcissist and the bad narcissist are fundamentally different in their intentions, they could belong to the same category. A good narcissist may be grandiose, and a bad narcissist may be vulnerable. Grandiose narcissists and vulnerable narcissists are both self-serving but express it in different ways.

NPD is incurable, but it's not untreatable. The only available treatment method for NPD is psychotherapy, and its success is contingent on the willingness and cooperation of the narcissist. This therapy is a long process. As a matter of fact, it takes years to see considerable change, if at all, in the narcissist.

The narcissist will have to be always encouraged and treated with love and care, as she could cancel her therapy at any time in a fit of narcissistic rage. NPD is especially difficult to treat because it involves a radical change in behavior. The likely unwillingness of the narcissistic patient to undergo therapy and the challenges of keeping them in therapy are the reasons why prognosis for NPD is not favorable.

With the knowledge you've gained so far in this book, you know that the chances for recovery for NPD are low—but treatment isn't impossible.

CHAPTER SEVEN

TAKING BACK YOUR POWER

This book wouldn't be complete without proven strategies on how to get yourself back together and take back your power. It's not an easy feat to be a victim of narcissistic abuse. So the fact that you're a survivor is impressive. You may not see it that way—that you're a survivor; you may laugh it off and object, "A survivor? But I'm barely surviving."

I still insist that you're way stronger than you think. You may have been broken, battered, and shattered, but you can rise again. You may have lost yourself, but you will find yourself. You may feel empty and exhausted, but hold on! You will be fulfilled.

I believe you can take back your power. I have faith in you that you can get yourself back together and live strongly. If I didn't believe in you, I wouldn't be sharing with you the following tested tips on how to get your life back together. I wouldn't even have bothered writing this book.

Here are the tips and strategies to taking back your power:

Seek Knowledge

I'm happy to tell you that you're already on the journey to get back your power. Yes, you are! By laying your hands on this book and reading it to this section, you already are on track to living your life peacefully. You're seeking knowledge. You're gathering information that will help you on your journey to fulfillment, to healing.

I'm sure already that some of your fears have already been allayed. You now have a clearer picture of yourself and your childhood experiences. The interesting thing is that you may not even have known what your mom's negative behavior was called, and why she's behaving that way.

What you knew before was that you just grew up with a mom who didn't care about you but only herself. But you're confident with your knowledge now that your mom was struggling with NPD. One can't solve a mysterious problem. So now that you know what the problem is, you will know how to tackle it. Though seeking knowledge is a good start, there's still more.

Befriend Reality

Now that you know what the problem is, you have to accept reality. It's good to think your narcissistic mom will change and come to give you all the care and love she owes you. I really wish that could happen, and I'm not being sarcastic. But it's a possibility—a greater one—that change may not happen for your mom.

My advice for you is don't expect your mom to change. Instead, be determined in your quest to be yourself. Your narcissistic mom won't change or may never change. Though these two statements look similar, they are fundamentally different.

"She won't change" means she doesn't want to change. Does the bad narcissist ring a bell? She's intentionally hurting you. She's deliberately violating your boundaries and belittling you. She hates your guts and will badmouth you whenever she has the chance.

The second statement, "She may never change," means that even if she's willing to change, she may find it difficult to. She's a good narcissist. Though she'll keep hurting you and crossing your boundaries, she's helplessly used to it.

When you accept that your narcissistic mom will never change her behavior, you'll become free and won't get so frustrated. Her actions and words won't be surprising or as painful as before. The narcissist may not change—that's the reality—but you can change how you respond to her.

It's better to accept that your mom can't change and move on with your life. And if she changes after releasing herself for psychotherapy, it's good for you. It won't be good for you to live in denial of reality. In fact, don't just accept reality but also befriend it. You'd be so surprised how this will make you feel better.

Set Boundaries

Don't be afraid to set physical and emotional boundaries. It's alright to set limits. Let your mom and others know the red lights. Every0ne has boundaries—even your narcissistic mom—and so should you. Boundaries help us define behavior and acts that are acceptable and unacceptable to us.

Setting healthy boundaries with your mom will give you a sense of self-esteem. I know it can be very difficult for a person who has suffered narcissistic abuse in the hands of her mom to assert boundaries now. This isn't going to be easy. I just have to be frank with you because I know how difficult it is for adult children who had a wonderful mother-child relationship to break away from their moms' influence, so it's twice as hard for those with a narcissistic mom.

But you just have to set boundaries. You need it for your mental wellbeing. And the earlier you start, the better for you. It's going to be especially difficult for you because the person you're setting the boundaries for doesn't recognize boundaries. Narcissists are boundary-blind folks, who don't care about anyone's boundaries.

Whether you like to admit it or not, you're more connected with your past than you want to admit. Your role in the family, either as the golden child or the scapegoat, has unconsciously defined you to be who you are today. As the golden child, you could've been used to please your mom and spent a lot of time seeking her love. But you've come to realize that you've lost a huge chunk of yourself in the process. Your sense of purpose has been terribly affected, and you feel drained and empty.

If this is your story, it's about time you asserted your boundaries with your mom. Let her know, even if she doesn't care, that you're an individual and that you have likes and dislikes, that you need some space to be your own person. Her response may be fiery or calm, but that's not important. What's important is that you've let her know, for the first time, perhaps, that you need to be yourself.

And if you're the scapegoat, who's borne the brunt of narcissistic abuse in the family, you should also set your boundaries. Actually, it's easier for you than for the golden child, because you've always been treated unfairly and harshly. But, as I've shown, you're also not exempt from the wrong influence of your narcissistic mom.

Your horrible experience with your mom has negatively affected your relationships. The constant violations of your boundaries by your mom could have discouraged you from setting boundaries in your other relationships. It's time you set those boundaries. This will give a nice feeling you never knew was possible.

What are those things that your mom does that really make you mad? What does she do that drives you crazy? These are the areas where you need to set boundaries. Stop ignoring your feelings. The more you know your feelings, the more effective you become in setting boundaries. Don't mince words. Be unequivocal when setting your boundaries. Makes sure your mom and those you're in a relationship with understanding that you'd appreciate their cooperation and respect with regard to the boundaries you've set.

Indulge your Feelings

I can't underscore this point enough. You're the only one who knows your feelings. Nobody else knows. Unfortunately, however, children of narcissists have learned to ignore their feelings as a means of defense and survival. But if you want to take back your power, you'll have to take back your feelings.

You may have unconsciously learned to ignore how you feel or even despise your feelings. I understand why you're used to ignoring your feelings. I know you had to ignore your feelings so that you could live in peace with your demanding mom. I also know that if you didn't ignore your feelings, it might have been hell.

Narcissists don't care about how other people feel, and they also make life miserable for those who hold on to their feelings. But if you want to escape the grip of your mom's narcissism, you have to indulge your feelings. You just have to. Once you're able to recognize your feelings, you're on your way to healing.

It may even be difficult for you to know your true feelings if your mom had gaslighted you to a great degree. You may be living with unoriginal feelings that aren't your own, feelings that you've been indoctrinated to believe are yours for years. You need to break free from these feelings.

But to break free from your unoriginal feelings, you'll have to listen to them. It's when you pay meditative attention to your feelings that you'll be able to know and separate feelings that aren't yours from the ones that are yours. You'll know your feelings, and they will set you free.

Go after your Dreams

Going after your dreams is a great service you do for yourself if you want to take back your power. Dreams are what make life meaningful. You should take your time to discover your dreams. You don't have to rush. As a victim of narcissistic abuse, it may be difficult for you to chase your dreams.

You may not even be motivated to dream because of the ordeals you've had to go through in your mom's hands. Failing to have dreams and go after them isn't good for self-esteem. It means you're still living in the cage your mom has placed you in. She is still holding you.

If you want to take back your power, you have to dare to dream and go after your dreams with passion. Stop making excuses for not having dreams. For how long will you keep accusing your mom of being responsible for your problems? For how long will you keep playing the victim card?

I'm not in any way suggesting that your mom is at fault because she is--she abused you during your childhood days. But I'm saying, let it go. Your bitterness is actually working more against you than it's working, if at all, against your mom. Think about it, does your narcissistic mom really care about feelings? Does she care about your bitterness? She doesn't care if you have dreams or not and don't expect her approval.

If you're an emotional wreck without dreams, it'll only reinforce your mom's belief that you're no good, and that she's always been right about you. You're an adult now, and it will be your fault if you don't move on with your life. And I'm sure the last you'll want to do is to justify your narcissistic mom.

So go ahead and dream. But it's not just enough to have dreams. In fact, having dreams is the easier part. Taking solid steps to make dreams happen is real work. This is where you have to set your passion free. You'll have to let go of self-pity and vulnerability if you want to be among the dream achievers.

I must be frank with you—making a dream become a reality isn't easy. It takes proactive and active efforts. It takes mental toughness. You have to be prepared to meet obstacles. Anyone dreaming without foreseeing obstacles on the way is bound to fail.

By the way, you should develop a healthy mentality about obstacles, because they aren't bad. It's also about your perception. You can see obstacles as springs that bounce you up toward your dreams or as landmines that blow your dreams up in your face. Your perception will either help you achieve your dreams or help you destroy them.

The greatest obstacle victims of narcissistic abuse have always faced is their mom. Children of narcissistic moms don't have favorable opinions about their moms. Their moms are their number one enemy when it comes to making progress. Their moms are the cause of their poor self-esteem, poor social relation, depressions, and every other bad thing about them.

This is very true. Narcissistic moms negatively affect their children even into adulthood. These negative influences are both direct and indirect. Your mother's unbelievable disgust and disbelief about your ability can deal a great blow to your self-confidence. This can directly discourage you from fighting for your dreams. The direct influences require you to have contact with your mom still.

But even if you're not living with your mom, she can still affect your mentality. The horrible seeds she has sown into you over the years can grow into big leafy trees, thereby preventing the sunlight of determination from reaching you. These are the indirect ways her thorns choking your dreams and determination.

I should let you know, however, that the greatest obstacle you'll face along the way to achieving your dreams won't be your mom, but you. You didn't expect that, did you? Your dreams are yours to make and go after. You have to refuse to be slowed down or impaired by your mom. Take yourself back from the snares of your past and dare to dream for the present and the future.

Stop Blaming

If you want to heal from the abuse of your mom, you have to stop blaming. You're most prone to blaming yourself. Your mom might have succeeded in painting you as the bad egg, the scapegoat. You have to stop carrying guilt for everyone. Don't blame yourself for your mom's failure, your sister's failure, or anyone's failure.

Your childhood has happened and there's nothing you can do about it. You have to come back from a guilt trip. Don't be hard on yourself. As you have now realized, narcissists are very good gas lighters. Your mom always accused you of causing her to do bad things. If she cursed you, you caused it. If she threw things at you, you made her do it.

She's gaslighting you. You didn't make her do any bad thing. She did those things because she wanted to. She did those terrible things because she loved to. She did those things because she wanted to dominate you. She did those things because she couldn't stand you being a success. She did those things because you were special! So wake up and stop falling for her trap.

If you want to be healed from your mom's abuse, you have to stop blaming yourself. You have to take it easy on yourself. Relax and take the load of blame and shame off your shoulders. You've carried it enough. Drop it and leave it for good.

It's not your fault. Don't be deceived! It's when you stop blaming yourself, your mom, or anyone that you'll be able to see the whole situation clearly. It's then you'll be able to heal perfectly.

Going "No Contact"

If you feel physical separation will help you feel better, please, by all means, move away from your mom. You don't have to feel bad about it. It's the best option for you. Distance will help you to relax and live your life. This may require you to change your phone contact, email, social media handle, or even your residence.

Why not, if it's worth the effort? Your peace of mind and sanity are priceless. This move could shock your mom, and she may react typically. It's even better if you only inform her after you've left. Don't disclose your location to her or to relatives you don't trust, as they may tell your mom. Be free like a bird. Only do this if you've been pushed to the wall and you think it's the best thing for you.

But like I've said before, physical separation from your mom is ineffective if you're still emotionally attached. I'm saying, there's no point if your mom isn't in your vicinity, but she's still in your head.

Go Grey!

However, if, for some reasons going no contact is not feasible, you will have to resort to what some have called the "grey rock method." This method encourages maintaining little communication with your abuser, in this case, your mom. If you're still living with her, try not to give her attention.

Be indifferent when answering her questions, and answer her in as few words as possible. When she shouts at you or call you names, try as hard as possible to hide your anger. Don't let her know she's got to you. You may even joke it off. If possible, don't let her know your moves and plans so that she won't use them against you.

This is what gray rock is all about. The idea is to do everything to make her lose interest in you. Grey method attempts to do away with all inflammables that can help your abuser explode. You have to be boring. Sound like you don't care about your mom's abuse. No matter how stinging her words her, don't show it.

It sounds simple, but you'll need to develop a thick skin. You'll need to be strong and determined. Don't give your mom what she wants. Don't give her that sad look she craves; don't let her see your tears; don't jump at once to do her biddings, but take your time.

She'll begin to lose interest in you. She'll find you boring and lifeless. As she's losing you, you'll be finding yourself. This is a method that's worth trying. By the way, this method is called "grey rock" because the grey rocks inspire it. You don't notice grey rocks because they don't call attention to themselves. So do everything with your mom in a way that you won't call attention to yourself.

Keep your Apology Brief

Keep your apology brief, or don't even apologize at all. Don't be generous in your apology. This may sound rude to the ears, but it's one of the steps you have to take if you want to take your power back from a narcissist. You see, apologies only make the narcissist stronger and more resolute in her belief that she's always right.

No matter how often you apologize to a narcissist, it will never be enough. Apologizing to a narcissist is like fetching water in a basket. Your apology means nothing to a narcissist. It may placate her for a while, but not forever. Be sure that the thing you apologized for will be referred to in the near future.

You may hear something like this, "That's what you did the last time too," "You're always fond of doing this," or "I forgave you the last time, and you're doing the same thing." You may apologize, but narcissists don't forget. I haven't said you shouldn't apologize, but keep it dry and short—don't be dramatic about it.

You also have to watch your apology because it may be that you're being gaslighted to apologize for what you didn't do. Don't underestimate the chicanery of a narcissist, especially the manipulative skills of your mom. Don't! One way to keep watch is to watch your apology.

Ask yourself these questions: "Do I really need to apologize?" "What am I to apologize for?" "How often have I had to apologize for this offense?" "Does this person accept apologies?" and other similar self-evaluating questions. You'll be able to know if you should indeed apologize or you're being manipulated to apologize. So apologize, if you really have to, in a way that doesn't feed the ego of your narcissist. You'll also not be giving her the chance to tell her stories or yell.

See a Psychotherapist

Ultimately, you'll have to see a psychotherapist. A psychotherapist is a psychologist who's trained to help people going through mental or emotional challenged discover the underlying cause of their challenges. She does this through talk. She may also have to prescribe drugs that can help with depression or insomnia.

This book is an informational guide and shouldn't replace psychotherapy. In fact, my purpose is to create awareness on what NPD is so that narcissists and victims of narcissism will be encouraged to go for psychotherapy. All I did was to make the work of the psychologist easier. The psychotherapy session will fast-track the healing process.

Chapter Summary

It's possible to take your power and life back from insecurity and imprisoning past. All hope isn't lost in your case, so don't lose hope. You deserve a good life like everyone else. You deserve to have great dreams and achieve them. You deserve to be free to be you.

So you need to pay attention to yourself.

Bond, with your feelings, understand the language of your feelings. Our feelings are honest advisers. They affirm our words. Even if we deceive ourselves with words, our feelings won't be carried away. How honest you are with your feelings will determine if you'll take back your power—if you will rediscover yourself.

The more you blame yourself, the more control she has over you, even remotely. Your refusing to accept reality is only make her venom more potent.

Limit your dealings with the narcissist in your life to the minimum as possible. If possible, stop interacting with the narcissist. Cut off means of communication with her. If you have to deal with them, deal with them intellectually, not emotionally. You'll make them feel great if you get emotional with them. Don't show that they hurt your feelings.

Keep dry eyes in their presence, even if you'll weep later. Let the narcissist know as little about you as possible. Have it in mind that they can use what they know about you against you in the future. She won't just let you be or go just like that. Expect a fight. Expect her to up the ante in her provocations.

Don't fall for her provocative baits. Be watchful and be in the game. Seeing the whole thing as a game will help you to cope better with her assaults. It will also help you to keep your emotions in check. I'll say again; it's not going to be easy.

If you can go no contact for you to have peace, please do so. And if at the moment you can't avoid your narcissistic mom, go grey!

Live as if you don't live in that house. Be deaf to her abusive words. Be blind to her incendiary actions.

Be the mature person. Going grey isn't easy, but it's worth the stress.

CONCLUSION

Thanks for getting this book and reading it to the end. I know you almost can't wait to share your knowledge about it with your family and friends. Now that you've learned more about NPD, its causes, and impacts—and specifically, you've understood the psychology of a narcissistic mom—you have been weaponized.

Whether you're a victim of NPD, or just an avid reader, or even a narcissist, you have been empowered with knowledge. Ignorance is no excuse. It's another situation entirely when you didn't know. Now that you know, you have to act, and you have to act fast.

I implore you to put the knowledge you've learned in this book to use. If you have to read it again (and please do), then do. You may not be a victim of narcissistic abuse, but you should be on guard around those who exhibit narcissistic signs. Don't let them manipulate you. Go grey!

I must reiterate—my aim in this book isn't to attack narcissists but to create awareness about NPD and help victims of narcissistic moms and narcissistic parents in general heal and find themselves again. I also want society to know what narcissism is and what it's not, and to have a greater awareness of it.

Exhibiting narcissistic traits inconsistently isn't narcissism, in the same way as being paranoid in some circumstances isn't a case of Paranoid Personality Disorder. There's no such thing as healthy narcissism—unless expression of one or two narcissistic traits is what is being referred to.

The negative influences narcissistic moms have on their children are undeniable. Children who suffered narcissistic abuse are pushed to adjust their personalities to accommodate the excess of their moms. They are forced to adjust their emotions and feelings to cope with the abuse.

This malignant adaptation shoves them to the extremes. They are either oversensitive or insensitive, either domineering or vulnerable, either thin-skinned or thick-skinned, either skeptical or gullible, etc. All this affects their social life, making it difficult to relate with others.

But they can get themselves back on course. Victims of abuse shouldn't give up. With the right measures, they can take back their power. They can be healed and be set free from the web of the ugly past. Healing is possible. Don't let anyone tell you it's not, and don't tell yourself that healing is an impossible task. People are healing, and so can you!

It's my passion to help spread the word about the ordeal victims of narcissistic abuse go through. I believe you can help victims of narcissistic abuse and even people with NPD with this book in your hand.

Newton's first law of motion is again vital in taking back your power. The law says, "An object will remain in a state of motion unless an external force acts on it." You'll remain depressed and frustrated unless you allow the force of what you've learned in this book to act.

Are you a victim of narcissistic abuse?

I want you to stay strong. Don't let your mom have the final say. Don't let her have a grip on you. Let go of the past and take hold of the now and the future. Know this: you continue to give your narcissistic mom control over you when you don't follow the strategies I've shared on how to take back your power.

But I'm confident that you will break free with the knowledge you've acquired in this book and learn to fly.

HELPFUL SOURCES

1. Diagnostic and Statistical Manual of Mental Disorders, 5th ed. (Washington: American Psychiatric Publishing, 2013).

2. Frederick S. Stinson et al. "Prevalence, Correlates, Disability, and Comorbidity of DSM-IV Narcissistic Personality Disorder: Results from the Wave 2 National Epidemiologic Survey on Alcohol and Related Conditions". The Journal of Clinical Psychiatry 69(7):1033-45 (July 2008).

3. Morgan, T.H. Experimental Zoology (New York, Macmillan, 1917).

4. Stangor, Charles and Walinga, Jennifer. Introduction to Psychology – 1st Canadian Edition. Victoria: B.C.: BCcampus (2014.) Open Textbook Project, 2014. https://opentextbc.ca/ introduction to psychology/.

5. Julie L. Hall. "The Narcissistic Family: Cast of Characters and Glossary of Terms." The Narcissist Family Files. January 2017. Narcissistfamilyfiles.com/2017/01/26/the-

narcissist-family-its-cast-of-character-and-glossary-of-terms/.

6. Lunbeck, Elizabeth. "The Americanization of Narcissism." Harvard University Press, 2014.

7. Lasch, Christopher. "The Culture of Narcissism: American Life in an Age of Diminishing Expectations." New York City: W.W. Norton & Company, 1979.

8. Skylar. "The Gray Rock Method of Dealing with Psychopaths." https://180rule.com/the-gray-rock-methid-of-dealing-with-psychopaths/

9. Greenberg, Elinor. "Are Narcissists Bad People?" Psychology Today. October 2018. https://www.psychologytoday.com/us/blog/understanding-narcissism/201810/are-nacissists-bad-people.

Printed in Great Britain
by Amazon

35468869R00097